monsoonbooks

Sorasing I[...] illiterate farming family in a remote Thai village. He was his parents' only child and, as was common in rural areas, was raised by his grandmother, leaving his parents free to labour all day in the rice paddies. At sixteen years old he became one of the youngest novice monks ever to be awarded the title Maha—Great—for his achievements in mastering the Pali language. Sorasing remained as a novice monk until he finished his high school studies, then disrobed to continue his education at tertiary level.

Peter Robinson ordained as a Buddhist monk in Thailand in 1993 and spent the following year in meditation in an isolated forest monastery. With the ordained name of Phra Peter Pannapadipo, he wrote four books, including *Phra Farang: An English monk in Thailand* and *Little Angels*. The royalties from his book sales were donated to a charity he created to award study scholarships to needy Thai youngsters. By 2010 the charity—The SET Foundation—had supported nearly 4,000 students through college or university. Peter disrobed from the monkhood in 2003 and now voluntarily devotes all his time to running the SET Foundation.

Other books by Peter Robinson
(Phra Peter Pannapadipo)

Phra Farang: An English Monk in Thailand
Published by Arrow Books

Little Angels
Published by Arrow Books

One Step at a Time
Published by Bamboo Sinfonia

Good Morning, Buddha
Published by Post Books

IN GRANDMOTHER'S HOUSE

THAI FOLKLORE, TRADITIONS AND RURAL VILLAGE LIFE

SORASING KAOWAI & PETER ROBINSON

monsoon

monsoonbooks

Published in 2011
by Monsoon Books Pte Ltd
52 Telok Blangah Road
#03-05 Telok Blangah House
Singapore 098829
www.monsoonbooks.com.sg

ISBN: 978-981-08-6658-7

Cover photo©Dallas & John Heaton, Photo Asia

Excerpts from *Phra Farang: An English Monk in Thailand* and *Little
Angels*, both published by Arrow Books, are reprinted by permission of
The Random House Group Ltd.

National Library Board, Singapore Cataloguing-in-Publication Data
Sorasing Kaowai, 1980-
In grandmother's house : Thai folklore, traditions and rural village life
/ Sorasing Kaowai and Peter Robinson. – Singapore : Monsoon Books,
2011.
p. cm.
ISBN: 978-981-08-6658-7 (pbk.)
1. Folklore – Thailand. 2. Thailand – Social life and customs.
3. Country life – Thailand. I. Robinson, Peter, 1947 July 31- II. Title.
DS568
390.09593 -- dc22   OCN663860716

Printed in Singapore
15 14 13 12 11   1 2 3 4 5

Dedicated to
Granny Say Krariangdee
1921–1991

Contents

GRANNY SAY KRARIANGDEE

Preface

Sorasing Kaowai:

This book is about the things my late grandmother taught me when I was a child, growing up in a remote little village in the Thai countryside from 1980–1993. Those were formative years for me, though my simple and traditional rural upbringing hardly prepared me for later, when I left the village to study in a big city. That was a shock. But although the two environments were so completely different, many of the things I learned from Granny during my village childhood proved to be of lasting value in my city adulthood. My long conversations with her about folklore, about the *right* way to do things, about the importance of the natural world and the need to preserve our traditions have stayed with me throughout my life. They always will, no matter where I live.

Although I only got to know Granny well during the latter period of her life, the years I spent with her came immediately before a time of almost revolutionary change in the lifestyle of rural Thai people. By the time Granny died in 1991, electricity had arrived in even the most remote villages, buffaloes were rapidly being replaced by mechanised farm equipment and modern chemical pesticides and fertilisers were available. In the same period, rural health clinics became widespread and villagers no longer had to rely on herbal medicines and traditional healers. Improvements in the education system had also reached right down to village level and many youngsters—including me—were leaving their little villages and the simple farming life for the opportunities of higher education and employment in the big cities. But with each advance, something else was lost. By just one generation or two after Granny's, villagers were considerably less self-sufficient and many of their traditional rural skills had been forgotten or discarded, instead of being passed on to the next generation. Many ancient animist beliefs and superstitions were also forgotten, except by the most elderly village folk.

Although my interest in folklore stems from my countless childhood conversations with Granny, there are other things included here too; things I have since discovered for myself. During my research, I spent some time talking with other very old country ladies—some of them much older than my granny—listening to their childhood memories and the things they remembered *their* grandmothers telling them. I am happy to record some of those memories.

I am sure there will be readers who know considerably more about Thai folklore, traditions and superstitions than I do and who may consider some of the content of this book to be inaccurate. Maybe so, but I have written about traditions as understood and practiced in *my* little village, which may have been different from how they were understood in some other regions.

I'm told my spoken English communication is quite good, but I know my written English is not. In preparing this book, I must acknowledge the enormous help I received from co-author Peter Robinson. Peter is a British long-term resident of Thailand and, as the former Buddhist monk Phra Peter Pannapadipo, a well known author in his own right. Peter tidied up my notes (which actually required considerably more than simply tidying up) and put my memories, research and words into a readable form. The writing style is Peter's, the memories are mine.

When Thai people perform a good action or some meritorious deed, they often dedicate the merit earned to a relative, living or dead. If there is any merit in this book, I dedicate it to my grandmother, who passed on some of her great wisdom and knowledge of Thai folklore to me.

Peter Robinson:

I've been resident in Thailand since the early 1990s. I lived for ten years as a Buddhist monk in several rural and city monasteries and now live as a layman in a big northern city.

After I left the monkhood I think that, like many long-term expat residents, after a few years I began to take my adopted country somewhat for granted. I became quite complacent, doing only those things I wanted to do, going only to the places I liked or needed to visit, eating the foods I most enjoyed or at least recognised, and forming most of my relationships with Thais who could speak at least some English. I started to ignore almost everything going on around me that I didn't understand or couldn't immediately relate to. After a while, I forgot what an exotic and fascinating place Thailand really is and it became simply the country I lived in. That's changed for me now, mainly because of my many conversations with Sorasing.

I met Sorasing in about 1998, when he was a novice and I was a monk. We were living at the same monastery. After we both disrobed from the monkhood we kept in touch, partly because he had been awarded a university scholarship by the SET Foundation, of which I was the founder. One day, while I was talking casually with Sorasing, he mentioned a superstition that his grandmother had told him about many years before, when he was a boy growing up in his village. It was a fascinating story and it led on to others, equally fascinating, and I realised he was a mine of information about Thai folklore, much of which had been passed on to him by his grandmother. With every story or anecdote he told me about life in the village, I wanted to know more. His stories almost immediately reawakened my interest in the country I am happy to call home and I became almost like an excited, wide-eyed, first-time visitor to Thailand again. Even something as simple as a walk through the local fruit market, a drive in the countryside or a visit to a little village monastery became full of renewed interest. I am very grateful for that.

I urged Sorasing to record some of things his granny had told him. *In Grandmother's House* is the result.

Sorasing and I usually communicate quite well but there may be a few instances in the book where I have misunderstood what he said or he has misunderstood what I have written. I don't think that's the case but if it is, the fault is entirely mine.

We have avoided using Thai words whenever possible, but given them when we think it is useful or interesting. There are several systems of transliterating Thai words into English and the results may vary considerably. For example, the Thai word for 'ghost' is sometimes written in English as *phee, phi* or *phii*. In this book, we have followed the official transliteration system provided to the authors by Associate Professor Supaporn Pornpibul, a teacher of English and the former vice-president of Rajabhat University in Nakhon Sawan. We are very grateful for her help and advice.

If, as Sorasing believes, merit can be passed on to others, living or dead, then I am also happy to dedicate mine to his grandmother. Thank you, Granny.

Living with Granny

My grandmother was a very wise and clever old lady. She was the village matriarch, herbal doctor, midwife and vet, but I don't mean she was wise or clever in an academic sense. Granny was completely illiterate. By wise, I mean the things she understood about folklore, about the healing plants that could be gathered in forest or field, about the habits of the animals, birds and insects which shared our environment, about village traditions and superstitions and the rural way of doing things—and why they were done that way. Granny was full of such wisdom; things she had learned from her mother and grandmother when she was a child and which had been passed down through countless generations, usually through the women folk.

Granny was especially knowledgeable about pre-Buddhist animist beliefs, spirits and ghosts. She accepted the reality of those things but she also seemed to be a very committed Buddhist, though her understanding of the Buddha's teaching was superficial at best. Granny seemed to find no conflict between her animist superstitions and Buddhist logic. Like all uneducated rural folk in her day, she had perhaps unconsciously taken and adapted aspects from each to form a hybrid belief system that suited her simple village and farming lifestyle. It's much the same today in rural areas.

Granny was the fourth of her parents' five children. She

was born in 1921 to an impoverished farming couple named Krariangdee. Her parents named her 'Say'. Medical centres and clinics were almost unknown in remote rural areas when Granny was born and the infant mortality rate was much higher than in modern times, but all her siblings survived to at least young adulthood. Large families were considered desirable then. Although having a large family obviously meant more mouths to feed, all food was grown or gathered freely in field and forest and nobody ever went hungry, however large the family. Having many children eventually provided more labour for the family rice paddies.

Granny's family lived in a remote little village named Ban Lao Pa Sa, in Uttaradit Province. The province is close to the border of Laos in Thailand's lower northern region. The community has grown in recent years but when Granny was a child there were about a hundred families in the village, living in crude houses or shacks made of wood and bamboo, with thatched roofs. Ban Lao Pa Sa wasn't a village in the Western sense, with all the houses gathered around a main street lined with shops. There was no main street and there were no shops. There were no streets or roads at all, just buffalo tracks, and the community was spread over a very wide area. Some families lived surrounded and isolated by their own paddy fields while others, like Granny's, lived within a small cluster of houses around the village monastery, quite far from the fields. The monastery was considered the village centre. The family had lived in the village for countless generations and I was born there too, in 1980.

The village was a peaceful and harmonious place in Granny's day, and even during my own childhood. Granny told me that during her lifetime, there hadn't been a single murder, rape, suicide or other violent crime in the village or surrounding community. Some of the men drank too much home-brewed rice whisky but drug abuse was unknown and even petty theft was rare. Things have changed now, of course.

In Granny's childhood years, Siam, as the country was then called, didn't have much of a formal or compulsory education system outside of Bangkok, especially for girls. Until about 1930, most rural primary and junior high schools were in the grounds of village monasteries with monks as the teachers, but only boys were allowed to study at the schools. The monk-teachers themselves were sometimes barely literate. Like her mother and grandmother before her, Granny had no formal education at all, not even a few years at primary school. She couldn't read or write or even speak modern Thai very well; she spoke only a local northern dialect. She couldn't even sign her own name. On the very rare occasion when she needed to sign a document, which was probably only once or twice in her life, she had to use a thumbprint.

Even if it had been available, the most basic education for rural folk in Granny's day was considered a waste of time and unnecessary for children who were going to labour in the rice paddies for the rest of their lives. Never mind about learning English, maths, geography, history, science or even the Thai language; rural folk generally were so poor (many still are) that everybody in the family had to help with the work, regardless of whether they were very young or very old. They usually carried on working till the day they died.

In modern times, many youngsters from impoverished rural families still receive only the most basic schooling, despite great improvements to the national education system. Six years of primary and six years of high school education are now theoretically compulsory and free, including the cost of books and uniform, but many rural families still can't afford the associated expenses of bus fares, school lunch, extracurricular activities and so on, and especially not the loss of a pair of helping hands from the paddy fields. Many children still drop out of the education system after the third year of high school, under pressure from their parents to contribute to the family income in some way. Some don't study at high school at all and instead start work in the paddy fields as soon as they finish their primary education.

Granny started fulltime work in the fields in 1930, when she was nine years old, though she had already been helping out with simple farming tasks for several years. At nine years old, her childhood days would have been considered at an end by her family and she was expected to work as hard as any adult. When they were in their teens and if they weren't needed to help in the fields, youngsters were often sent by their parents to work as building labourers, rickshaw drivers, maids or in other unskilled jobs in the cities, sending money home each month, but Granny spent her entire life working in the fields.

Granny rarely ventured beyond the outskirts of the village, but she had no reason to. Getting out of the village was anyway very difficult throughout her lifetime. Nobody in the village owned a car or motorbike and the only form of transport was a buffalo cart. The nearest proper road could only be reached from the village by a twelve-kilometre buffalo track. The track was deeply potholed in the dry season and often underwater in the rainy season, so the village was sometimes cut off entirely from the rest of the world. After reaching the village from the road, the track dribbled off into a deep forest which surrounded the community on three sides. Uttaradit City, which is only about twenty-five kilometres from the village, was a major and difficult excursion at any time of the year. Granny made the ten-hour round trip only a few times in her life. She didn't like or understand the city anyway because the crowds, traffic and noise were all very confusing for her. Even I visited the city only two or three times before I left the village permanently in 1993, when I was thirteen years old. By that time the buffalo track had been replaced by a paved road and a city bus passed within a few kilometres of the village, but I couldn't afford the bus fare.

There was little or no mechanical equipment in the village in Granny's day and farming was back-breaking work. Digging irrigation channels in the paddy fields, hoeing the land, guiding a heavy, wooden, buffalo-drawn plough through the deep mud, bending to plant rice seedlings, harvesting with sickles and threshing and milling the rice all had to be done by hand. In my own childhood years through the 1980s, my parents followed exactly the same methods and did everything by hand, as did all the farmers in the village. If you take a drive through remote rural communities, you will still see a few very old ladies bent almost at right angles from the waist and unable to straighten up, their spines permanently damaged from a lifetime spent bending to work in the paddy fields. Granny was afflicted in the same way and suffered back pains and walking difficulties throughout her life, especially as she got older.

Despite the hard work involved, Granny loved working on the land and being close to it. She seemed to have a genuine and natural affinity to all growing things. I often saw her take a handful of rice or a piece of fruit, examine it closely, and then smile. Just a few weeks before she died—and she knew she was dying—she asked me to help her walk to the paddy fields. She was quite frail by then and it was a long and difficult walk for her. When we got there, she simply stood and looked around at the rice plants, with a contented and happy smile on her face. That was the last time she ever saw her paddy fields. I wish I could have taken her photograph at that moment.

As far as I know, Granny was photographed only once in her life. Ordinary people didn't have cameras then and paying for a studio photograph was out of the question, unless it was for a very special occasion. Sometimes a travelling photographer would pass through the village, offering his services for ten baht for one photograph, but that was a lot of money in those days. Older people didn't like being photographed anyway. The only time a portrait photograph was usually displayed was at a person's funeral, so elderly people thought it was very unlucky to have their photograph taken, since they believed it tempted fate.

The only photograph I've traced of Granny was taken by a travelling photographer when she was about sixty. I would guess that it was actually taken in 1981 on her sixtieth birthday, since Thai people measure life in twelve-year cycles and the fifth cycle (sixty years) is an important one. It's a pity that Granny looks so stern and unsmiling in the photograph because that's not how I remember her at all, but I expect she was very nervous. I remember Granny as usually smiling or laughing, except when she was scolding me, which was quite often but always with good reason.

Despite looking a bit grumpy in the photograph, I remember Granny in her later years as being a striking-looking woman, though a bit on the stout side. Even though her crippled back meant she couldn't stand upright or walk very well, she had a quiet dignity about her, as have many elderly Thai ladies. Her dignity was natural but also reflected her position as village matriarch.

Matriarchs weren't appointed; the position came gradually and naturally with age, experience, wisdom and acquired respect. All the villagers respected Granny and as matriarch she was *expected* to be always dignified, always calm and to set an example to others. She usually was. If taken out of her village environment she would have been shy and confused, but within her own little community she was very confident. She had a definite 'presence' at any village gathering and people listened very attentively when she spoke or offered advice. But woe betide anybody who upset her or spoke or acted in some way that Granny thought was inappropriate to our village way of life or customs. Then she would become the fully fledged matriarch. She would never get angry or raise her voice; a slight pursing of the lips and a heavy, disapproving silence were quite enough to make her displeasure known. Despite her apparent toughness and occasional hardline attitude, she also had a very gentle and caring side to her personality, especially when it came to children and animals. That's the side of her that I remember most, and very fondly.

Besides being as mentally tough an old lady as you are ever likely to meet, I also remember Granny as being physically very strong; certainly as strong as any of the village men. Despite her damaged back, even when she was quite elderly she could still heft a heavy basket of rice or guide a plough through the thick, squelching mud of the paddy fields.

Granny's face and skin were dried and wrinkled from a lifetime spent working in the fields but I remember her eyes were as sparkly as a young girl's, especially when she and my mother were sharing a juicy piece of village gossip, screeching with laughter while they did so. They always seemed to be laughing about something, though as a child I rarely knew what it was. When she was laughing, Granny seemed almost beautiful to me, despite her strange make-up technique. Granny never once in her life used ordinary Western-style cosmetics. They weren't available in the village then but, like most of the women, she smeared white chalk powder on her face which gave some protection from the sun, ants and mosquitoes. A white skin was also considered attractive for women, though the chalk was very roughly and unevenly smeared on with the fingers, giving an odd streaky appearance. Her white face was starkly contrasted by her bright red lips, permanently stained from a lifetime of chewing betel leaves and areca nut. Granny would never have got the hang of Max Factor.

Just above Granny's top lip was a prominent dark mole, the sort of thing that might be considered an unattractive disfigurement by Westerners, but not to Thais. In Thai folklore, every mole or birthmark has a very precise meaning, depending on its position. Marks on the face, or on any other part of the body, are used by fortune tellers to predict the future or explain the character of a person, in the same way that palm lines are used.[1] Granny once told me, with a smile, that her mole meant that she liked art and literature (she couldn't read) and that she would marry a wealthy, well-educated man (her husband was impoverished and illiterate). The mole also meant she would be very talkative. The last bit, at least, was correct.

Granny had a lovely and often-seen smile, despite an obvious lack of teeth. She had never visited a dentist in her life. When she was a girl, and even an elderly lady, there wasn't a dentist within many kilometres of the village and she had no money for treatment anyway. Granny's few remaining teeth were not good but they were always very clean. Like everybody in the village, she made her own toothbrushes from twigs of the Khoi tree. Granny would chew the end of a twenty-centimetre-long twig until it became soft and fibrous, then brush it across her teeth, with a little rock salt added. Khoi also strengthens the teeth and gums and Granny frequently used the wood in some form in her herbal remedies, particularly for oral problems. The Khoi tree is also known as the Siamese Rough Bush or Toothbrush Tree *(Streblus asper)*. Its twigs have been used for dental hygiene in Southeast Asia for thousands of years. Recent scientific research has shown that traditional herbal healers, like Granny, knew what they were doing and that parts of the tree help control bacteria linked to dental decay and other oral infections.

The feature I remember most clearly about Granny is her hair. It was black, streaked with grey, and very long and silky. Granny never once in her life used modern shampoos. Instead, she would take four kaffir limes and roast them on a charcoal fire until the green skins turned brown. She would then cut each lime in half and rub it into her wet hair, leaving the juice to soak in for a few minutes before rinsing off. She combed her hair with a homemade wooden comb. Granny's hair was always very soft and shiny and had a beautiful lemony smell. Even today, whenever I smell a lemon or lime, I am reminded of her hair.

Like everybody else in the village, Granny always wore the same simple and traditional northern-style clothes. When working in the paddy fields, she wore a collarless, long-sleeved cotton shirt, buttoned at the front, with a calf-length cotton skirt, hitched up to make something like pantaloons. The men wore a similar shirt fastened with cloth ties and toggles, with elbow-length sleeves, and calf-length wrap-around cotton pants. The clothes were handmade in the village from local cotton and were always dark blue, the cloth being dyed with local indigo. The men also wore a multi-coloured rectangular length of cotton cloth tied around the waist. When working in the fields, the cloth could be wrapped around the head like a turban, giving some protection from the sun. The women usually wore conical homemade bamboo or palm leaf hats.

Although village women were always clean and tidy when they were not up to their knees in mud in the fields, none of them cared very much about their personal appearance at home. The idea of 'fashion' or 'style' would have been laughable in the village then, and still is. When not working in the fields, Granny always wore a pink or white lacy, short-sleeved blouse (sometimes with a bra worn on the outside) and a brightly patterned cotton sarong, made on her own loom. The sarong was held up just by a complicated fold and a knot, but for her frequent visits to the village monastery a fancy silver-alloy belt was added. Granny never owned a pair of shoes and was usually barefoot, but she sometimes wore an old pair of rubber flip-flop sandals. She would often have a length of 'sacred' white *sai sin* cotton string tied around her neck or wrist, given to her as a blessing by the abbot of the monastery. Sai sin is used in all Buddhist ceremonies and blessings and is worn until the string drops off or rots. Granny usually wore no jewellery but she had pierced her ears herself and on very special occasions wore a pair of tiny gold earrings, given to her by my grandfather as a wedding present.

Granny's only surviving childhood friend (she was ninety years old when I talked to her) told me that Granny was very slim, attractive and vivacious in her late teens and that several young men in the village hoped to win her hand. Although she seems to have been a lively and fun-loving girl, Granny would never have gone out on a 'date'. There was nowhere to go anyway but it simply wasn't done in the village then and her parents would never have allowed their daughter to be alone with any unrelated man. Courtship would have been slow and discreet and very closely watched by the parents, as well as the village elders. Any young man who saw Granny as a prospective partner would perhaps try to arrange to sit close to her at village gatherings, or would coincidentally be walking home from the paddy fields at the same time as Granny and her girlfriends. Shy smiles and subtle signals would have been given and returned but there would *never* have been any sort of physical contact, not even a holding of hands. Eventually the young man would have had a quiet word with his father, who would have had a quiet word with Granny's father, and an understanding would have been reached.

Granny married a local man named Janta Jakpajook in 1941, when she was twenty years old. Janta was also twenty and came from an equally impoverished and illiterate background. In some ways it was a marriage of convenience. With no other options, they both had to try to make a living from the land. Having a partner to share the burden made things easier but I'm sure they loved each other in a typically understated Thai way. After she was married Granny kept her own surname, though her children took her husband's name, as was traditional then. Granny and her husband were born in the same village and had known each other since they were children. They were well-suited and it was probably inevitable that they would marry, since there wasn't a wide choice of potential partners in the small community and nobody thought to look further afield. Granny was a local girl and would marry a local boy. Marrying quite young meant the opportunity to start raising a family early on and Granny seems to have been determined to have many children. She had eight.

Marriages weren't arranged in a formal sense but the two fathers would certainly have discussed it at length before giving their consent. Amongst other things, they would have negotiated the size of the dowry to be paid. Unlike in some other cultures, in Thailand the man gives a dowry to the woman, rather than the other way round. This dowry is sometimes known as *paying for the mother's milk*: the cost to the parents of bringing up the prospective bride since childhood. In the village it was traditional that the dowry would usually include a gift of gold and an agreed amount of money. Grandfather gave a pair of gold earrings and probably two hundred baht in cash. That was a huge amount then for an impoverished farmer and he had certainly been saving towards his dowry all his working life. To give an idea of the true value of the cash dowry, Granny's childhood friend told me that as a farm labourer she then earned only fifty satang a day—a half of one baht. The cash would have been returned by Granny's parents to the newlyweds as a wedding gift to help get them started. In rural areas at the time the dowry might also include a buffalo or other farm animals, but Granny's friend told me that my grandfather didn't make such gifts.

For poor rural people, getting married meant little more than setting up home together, usually after having offered breakfast to the monks from the village monastery and receiving a blessing in return. There was little or no fuss and there is no formal marriage ceremony in Buddhism, but there were and still are many animist and Brahmin traditions involved which people usually follow, though the roots and meanings of the traditions have largely been forgotten. In modern times, more people formalise their marriage by registering it at the local town hall, but my grandparents never did.

Village children weren't allowed to attend weddings in Granny's day, nor in my own childhood. Parents were very protective and didn't want their children exposed to anything that might lead them to ask *why* the couple was getting married, what happened *afterwards* and *where did babies come from?* I didn't know anything about that sort of thing until I was about thirteen years old. As an adult I have attended many weddings, including a few in the village, and I know Granny's wedding ceremony would have followed many centuries-old customs.[2]

Separation or divorce was also very informal in Granny's time. The couple would simply go their own ways, but permanent separation in the village was very rare then. Once married, people usually stayed together through good times and bad, though they had little practical choice. If a couple wanted to part, that didn't cause the sort of problems that a modern separation or divorce can do. A poor couple probably had little or no land of their own, their house was usually no more than a bamboo shack and they had nothing valuable to be argued about or fought over in court.

After they were married, Grandfather set to work to build a house for him and Granny to live in. There were no power tools in the village so Grandfather and a few helpful neighbours built the house entirely by hand, using little more than an axe, a saw and a hammer. It was the tradition in the village then that everybody helped out with such work, happily giving their labour free because they knew that one day they would themselves need help. They could only work on the house during slack times in the paddy fields, so it was nearly two years before it was finished. They did everything themselves, including chopping down hardwood trees in the forest, sawing the massive trunks into long planks, hauling the planks by buffalo cart from the forest to the site and then fitting them to the house. The house had only one room and was a large but ramshackle place, made from hardwoods like teak, as well as bamboo and other natural materials collected in the forest. Teak trees were very common then and it was still legal to cut them. Because the materials and labour were entirely free, even impoverished couples were able to build quite large houses and usually did, because they expected to have many children.

Although village houses were nearly always just one big room, that didn't cause any problems for large families. People respected each other's privacy and, if necessary, the room could be divided with curtains or bamboo screens. In Granny's day unmarried children usually stayed with their parents, so at one time there would have been ten people in my grandparents' house, but Granny loved being surrounded by her family.

Like most rural houses then and now, my grandparent's house was raised about three metres above the ground on many thick wooden posts as a protection from flooding and dangerous creatures, especially snakes. Broad wooden steps with no handrail led from the ground up to the living accommodation. The house originally had a traditional thatched roof made from two-metre-long panels of dried grass, about ten centimetres thick. Thatch needs to be renewed every two or three years, so Grandfather later replaced it with a 'modern' tiled roof, making the thin crude tiles himself using very fine clay made with dirt taken from abandoned termite mounds. The house had no bathroom and no running water and was poorly lit by several kerosene lamps. Electricity didn't arrive in the village until 1984. Even after the arrival of electricity, nobody in the village could afford to buy an electric fan, so the upper part of the house was always stiflingly hot in the daytime and was used mainly as somewhere secure to sleep at night. Village houses then usually had no windows but the many gaps between the uneven wall planks allowed an air flow through the room.

The large bare dirt area beneath raised houses makes a convenient but smelly pen for pigs or buffalo or, if there are no animals, simply a cool place to sit, or for an afternoon siesta. The space beneath my grandparent's house was the main living accommodation and all activities, apart from sleeping, took place there. Granny also used the space as a work area, where she made bamboo baskets, weaved cotton or prepared her herbal medicines, usually sitting on a wide and rickety bamboo platform, like a day bed.

Upstairs, there was no furniture in the house except for a wooden storage cabinet, which Grandfather made himself. An absence of furniture didn't mean the family was poor. Even in my childhood, none of the houses in the village had furniture because we didn't need it; our lives were lived almost entirely at floor level so chairs, tables and beds were unnecessary. There were no wardrobes because we had little more than the clothes we stood up in. The few spare clothes we had were simply piled on the floor or left hanging on a bamboo pole outside. When relaxing, eating or doing small tasks, we sat on homemade bamboo mats on the floor. We slept on the floor on the same mats, beneath cotton mosquito nets. Even now, most rural houses have little or no furniture, though these days there will usually be a television and maybe a refrigerator, proudly and prominently displayed in an otherwise almost empty room.

The only ornamentation in Granny's house was an out-of-date

calendar, hanging respectfully very high up on a wall. It showed a picture of a handsome and very young King Bhumibol Adulyadej, the present monarch. Although the King must have seemed a very remote figure to Granny, she revered him throughout her life, as did everybody in the village. Also high up on a wall was a shelf holding a small, brass Buddha image (quite an ancient one) with two candlesticks and a brass incense holder.

Granny cooked on an earthenware brazier in the open area beneath the house, using charcoal which she made herself from wood collected in the forest. The charcoal had the benefit of giving off a lot of smoke when first lit. The thick smoke drifted up into the house and kept mosquitoes away, as well as helping to prevent termites from making their nests in the wood. All the women in the village cooked in the same way and many still do, though bottled gas is now also widely used. Charcoal was prepared in a small homemade brick kiln, situated as far as possible from the house, as a fire precaution.

Although her cooking arrangements may seem primitive, Granny was a very good cook and was able to produce several different foods every evening within about thirty minutes, all made from entirely fresh ingredients. When I lived with Granny in my childhood, I never once ate any food from a tin, jar or packet, nor anything containing chemical additives, colours, preservatives or toxic pesticide residue. There were no shops in the village then but even if there had been, the idea of buying ready-prepared food from a shop would have seemed very strange to Granny.[3] The fields and forests supplied everything we needed.

After meals it was my duty to wash the dishes. The ancient iron pots and pans were scrubbed with charcoal ash and coconut fibre, though periodically I had to scour them in a nearby river, using coarse sand. Plates were cleaned with kaffir limes, cut in half, which besides getting the plates clean also gave them a fresh lemony smell. We didn't use knives and forks, just cheap pressed-tin soup spoons, painted green and with very rough and sharp edges. I didn't learn how to use a knife and fork until I was in my mid-teens.

Showering was done outside in the open, using unfiltered rain water. During the rainy season, water ran off the roof into pipes and then into several huge, covered, glazed stoneware jars, called *ong*, to be stored for later use. When the jars were nearly empty, they had to be topped up with water carried from the village well in heavy buckets. That was also one of my chores. During times of water shortage, which were frequent in the hot season, a dip in the local canal or a nearby stream had to suffice, despite the inconvenience of blood-sucking leeches. For modesty when showering, Granny wore a thin cotton sarong, hitched up above her chest and tightly tied. She didn't use soap when she bathed because she said there was no point, the water from the canal wasn't very clean, but after bathing she would dust her body with white chalk powder and cumin. Once a week she would also vigorously rub herself down with coconut fibre, to scour her skin.

The toilet was situated as far as possible from the house and was simply a hole in the ground, with a plank across it for sitting on and some very thin slivers of bamboo or strips of coconut fibre for cleaning with afterwards. The toilet room was enclosed by thin bamboo walls and a door, and with a thatched roof. Every so often, a new hole had to be dug and everything moved to the new location. That was considered very sanitary and modern, since most people used the nearest bush.

Laundry was usually done in the canal, but Granny didn't use detergent, which wasn't available in the village then. Our clothes were usually filthy from working in the muddy paddy fields, but the point was mainly to get the sweat out of them. A good soak in water with kaffir limes added, followed by a scrubbing with coconut fibre or a stone was usually sufficient.

Granny's house had no garden, apart from a small plot for herbs. Rural families didn't usually have gardens in the ordinary decorative sense, preferring well-swept dirt. Shrubs and low plants can provide convenient and cool hiding places for snakes, spiders, scorpions and other dangerous creatures. Although she had no garden, when Granny was first married she planted some carefully chosen trees near the house. Some provided fruit like mango, banana and jackfruit, some provided ingredients for her herbal preparations or cloth dyes and some were simply considered lucky or auspicious to have growing nearby.

Close to the house were my grandparents' two small rice stores. In modern times, the rice crop is usually stored in wooden or corrugated metal sheds but Granny's stores were handmade by my grandparents from tightly woven bamboo. The stores were dome shaped, about two metres tall and three metres in diameter, with flat tops. The top part or lid of the dome could be taken off when new rice grains were poured in at the end of the harvest. When rice was needed, someone would climb into the store through the top and pass out the rice in a bamboo basket. The stores were set on square wooden bases, then raised on posts to about one metre above the ground, to protect the rice from rodents. The space beneath, enclosed with a bamboo lattice fence, made a convenient chicken coop or a place to store fuel wood. Additional protection for the rice from rodents and damp was provided by spreading a thick layer of mud over the bamboo, made from liquefied buffalo dung mixed with rice husks. The mud dries to a very hard glaze. When I was a child, I helped my mother mix and spread the same sort of mud to protect our own small rice store. Bamboo rice stores are rarely seen anymore, except in the most remote villages.

Next to the rice stores was the spirit house; the home of the spirit which lived on that piece of land before the family house was built. In modern times spirit houses are usually very ornate and brightly coloured, made of painted concrete or expensive woods, but like most of those in the village Granny's was simple and unadorned, made from a large, rusty, square tin can. Spirit houses usually stand on wood or concrete posts, but Granny had set hers on top of a metre-high termite mound. To her, such mounds had great spiritual significance. Despite its simplicity, the spirit house provided a home for the guardian spirit and each day Granny would leave water, rice, incense and flowers there and say a little prayer for the spirit's continued benevolence.

In Granny's day, villagers were very hospitable to strangers and outside every house, or in the space beneath it, there was always a large, covered earthenware jar full of water, with a cup made from half a coconut shell and with a long bamboo handle, so thirsty passers-by could help themselves to a drink. Such jars and such hospitality are rarely seen anymore, even in my village.

My grandparents lived comfortably and happily together in their house for more than thirty years, until Grandfather died of cancer in 1971, when he was fifty. I hadn't been born then so I know little about him and nobody in the village now remembers him very well. Granny was fifty when her husband died but despite her various developing ailments, she was still willing and able to labour in the paddy fields all day. She was a very determined lady

Ate organic food but died of cancer at 50 -!

33

and it would take a very serious illness indeed to stop her from working. My parents' one-room house was on the same plot of land as Granny's, so after Grandfather died my mother was able to take care of Granny, at least as much as the very independent old lady would allow.

I was born nine years after Grandfather died, when Granny was fifty-nine and my mother was twenty-six. At home there was my granny, my father, my mother and I. We had only a small area of paddy field and cultivated just about enough rice each year for our own consumption. Besides rice we grew spring onions, beans and other vegetables and kept a few scrawny free-range chickens for eggs. My parents also worked as labourers in wealthier neighbours' fields. That provided almost the family's only cash income—just a few baht a day—but we were occasionally able to sell some of our vegetables. My father drank too much rice whisky and preferred not to work very hard, so there was never much spare money to buy luxuries, like meat. Almost the only meat the family ate regularly was rats, caught in the paddy fields. Eating rat wasn't itself an indication of poverty or starvation. All our food was caught or gathered in field or forest and included small birds and animals, snakes, lizards, fish, insects, plants and fruits. Even in modern times, the fields and forests are still a major source of food, fuel, building materials and herbal medicine for rural families.

Although my family was financially poor, we were never hungry. As a child, I helped with the gathering of food and became very clever at hunting small animals for the pot with my homemade catapult, a skill learned from my father. I would also sometimes go to the paddy fields in the evenings with a gang of other village boys to catch frogs and eels to eat, being careful not to disturb other night-hunters, like snakes. Granny once warned me that an eight-metre-long python had been seen in one of the fields—a snake easily capable of swallowing a small child like me.

Because Granny lived next door, she was part of the background of my life and I spent as much time in her house as I did in my own. From the day I was born, she took over most of the duties of motherhood from my mother, who had to work in the fields with my father from dawn till late afternoon almost every day. The only real break for my parents was the three days of the traditional Thai New Year holiday (*Songkran*) in April. It was and still is very common in rural areas for grandparents to take full responsibility for their grandchildren, leaving the parents free to work, either in the fields or as labourers in the faraway cities. Granny herself had been brought up as a child mainly by her own grandmother. Granny and I were together nearly all the time. When I was a baby she would rock me in my cradle, singing ancient northern-dialect lullabies which she had first heard as a baby from her own granny.

My cradle was carved from a single heavy piece of hardwood, like a dug-out canoe, suspended with thick homemade ropes from a ceiling beam beneath Granny's house. The sides and bottom of the cradle were about six centimetres thick. Although it would originally have been quite crudely carved, the cradle had been in use in my family for hundreds of years. My mother, granny and *her* granny had all been nursed in the same cradle. By the time I was rocked in it, the wood was polished as smooth as glass and was black and shiny with age. After I was old enough to walk, the cradle was passed on to a newborn baby in another branch of the family. I wouldn't be surprised if it's still in use today, though I haven't been able to locate it in the village.

As I got a little older, Granny would sometimes take me with her to the fields in a bamboo basket, leaving me sleeping but carefully watched in the shade of a tree while she worked nearby with my parents. As a toddler I joined Granny and my parents in the fields, trying to do whatever I thought might be helpful and, at the same time, learning my farming skills. By the time I was five or six years old, I probably knew more about growing rice and vegetables than any adult city dweller. That was my training period because it was fully expected by all the family, including me, that I would start fulltime work in the fields by the time I was about ten or eleven years old. I loved working in the fields with Granny and my parents because it gave us a real, though unacknowledged, sense of unity and of family; working together all day and then returning home exhausted to prepare and eat the evening meal together.

As Granny became older and gradually more unwell, our roles were slowly reversed and it was mostly me that cared for her. I prepared her meals, massaged her aching legs or, under her instruction and watchful eye, mixed herbs and roots to make hot compresses to ease the pain in her back. But despite our daily close contact and the great affection and respect I felt for her, I was very wary of Granny and sometimes even a little scared of her. Although she was usually very cheerful and never showed real anger, she could occasionally be quite grumpy and was quick to scold me. I had to be very careful how I spoke to her sometimes. I recall when I was about seven years old innocently asking what her maiden name was, though I can't imagine now why I wanted to know. Granny had a very strict and traditional sense of propriety and became seriously annoyed with me, declaring that no child had a right to ask such a question of someone older.

I didn't discover that she kept her maiden name after she was married until many years later, when I started researching her background.

I learned good manners and proper behavior from Granny very early on in my childhood. It's traditional in Thailand that a person's head must never be higher than the head of someone senior or in a socially superior position, so I had to duck mine a little whenever I passed Granny, even though as a child I was much shorter than her anyway. The same rule applied to any other adult or older person that I needed to pass. I could also never sit in a higher place than Granny and when sitting on the floor I had to be very careful that my feet never pointed in her direction. I always had to tuck them well under my body and never sit with my legs splayed out. The feet are considered by Thais to be the spiritually lowest and dirtiest part of the body and must never be pointed at people or, especially, towards Buddha images. The same rule about feet applies when food is set out on the floor. It's considered very bad manners to step over it. Each morning, at the first moment I saw her, I would *wai* Granny and greet her formally and politely. She would respond just as politely, though not wai to me in return. The wai is the beautiful Thai hand gesture which can show respect, courtesy, recognition, welcome or thanks, but it's more involved than it looks. The wai is made by joining the palms together, prayer-like, inclining them slightly inwards towards the chest and then slowly raising them to a point between the chest and the forehead. *Which* point the hands are raised to is very important and can make the wai either beautiful and well-received or, sometimes, an insult. The higher the hands are raised, the more respect is intended, but to raise them *too high* in an inappropriate situation or to an inappropriate person can cause embarrassment to that person. To raise them *too low* can also cause embarrassment. A younger person should always wai an older person first, and to a high level, and then the older person will return the wai, usually at a lower level. The height the hands are raised to signifies the relative age, rank, or social position of the two people, something which Thais seem to intuitively know. Children should always wai an adult, but the adult does not usually return the wai to a very young child. The only people who do not return a wai are monks. Even His Majesty The King will wai a monk, but the monk does not wai the King

Granny was very much the matriarch in the family, as well as in the village. All Thai people are taught to respect the older members of the family and elder people generally, so to me Granny was an authoritarian figure to be feared, even more than my father. For my family Granny was a great and constant presence in our lives and our little world revolved around her. Her word was law and we didn't dare disagree with her, even when she was quite obviously in the wrong. Perhaps I make Granny seem like some sort of ogre, but she wasn't at all. She simply believed in following tradition and the way that she had been brought up as a child. In her old age, she therefore believed it was her *right* to be treated with respect by anybody younger than her. Although she stood for no nonsense from anybody, she was also a constant comfort and support to us in times of trouble. She was always the first person I turned to if I had a fight with another village boy, or a problem at school. She was always there for me, usually sitting beneath the house in the late afternoon or early evening, muttering to herself while she wove very intricate bamboo baskets, or working at her cotton loom. After finishing my daily chores, I loved to sit and chat with her and that became part of our daily

e mail dave 30/1/11

routine for several years.

The cycle of our days was very simple, exactly as it had been for rural folk for centuries. Time measured in minutes, hours or even days meant very little to us. Every day was a working day and we had no concept of 'weekend'. Until I started attending primary school even I didn't know, or care, what day of the week it was. Granny quite likely never even knew the names of the days of the week and had no reason to know. Her reckoning of the passing of time was based around the weekly *Wan Phra* (Monk Day) when the monks didn't walk on their daily alms round and instead Granny took food to the local monastery.

Nobody in the family owned a watch and we had no clock, but Granny, Father and Mother couldn't tell the time anyway. I didn't learn until I started going to primary school. It took me nearly a year to understand time Thai-style, since I was so unfamiliar not only with clocks but even with the concept of 'time' when used to split up the day into shorter periods.[4] But in the village we didn't need clocks: we had no appointments to keep or schedules to meet and time for us followed the natural rhythms of the day. It was time to get up when the cock crowed at dawn and it was time for lunch when we heard the pounding of the monastery drum, calling the monks for their last meal of the day. It was time to sleep when the sun went down.

The adults usually left for their day's labour in the fields at about 6 am. Just before then, the bells of the village monastery would ring out to let us know that the monks were about to walk on their alms round.[5] Every day, regardless of the weather, Granny would wait bare-footed outside the house for the monks to walk in a silent line through the village. They would stop outside the house, raise the lids of their alms bowls and Granny would gently

39

and reverently place a spoonful of rice into each, sometimes with some curry or fruit, and then squat in the dust or mud while the monks quietly chanted a blessing. The food Granny offered was never leftovers; it was always freshly cooked that morning and was often better than the food we ate ourselves. For Granny, there could be no better way to start the day than with an act of generosity or compassion. On the weekly Monk Day, Granny would take food to the monastery and listen to long sermons about the Buddha's teaching. As she got older, she became very serious about 'making merit' and doing good deeds in that way, perhaps wanting to accumulate more merit to help her towards a better next life.

Our evenings were spent with small chores: repairing farm equipment, cotton weaving, washing our work clothes, making bamboo baskets, de-husking corn, peeling tamarind and other seasonal fruit, or preparing vegetables for the next day's breakfast. Everybody was asleep soon after nightfall and it was unusual to see a light burning in any house in the village later than that. We went to bed early because we had to rise very early, to get as much work as possible done in the fields before the day became too hot.

We also went to bed early because apart from chores and chatting, there was absolutely nothing else to do. We didn't have books, magazines or newspapers in the house because neither my parents nor Granny could read and we had no television or radio until 1987, when I was seven years old. Until then, we were almost totally cut off from anything happening in the world outside the village. We weren't very interested anyway. Years earlier, even WWII seems to have passed the village by almost unnoticed. After I started going to primary school I asked Granny what she knew about the war. She said she had heard there had been a war but she didn't know which countries were involved, why it started, when it ended or who had won.

Considering our almost cashless situation, it's odd that we were the first family in the village to have a television. I don't know where my father got it from, but it was pretty hopeless anyway. It was very old with a tiny black and white screen and could receive just one channel, and that only intermittently. Father had to rig up an aerial on the roof, supported by a five-metre-long bamboo pole, but he spent more time sitting on the roof turning the aerial this way and that to get a better signal than he spent actually watching the television. When it did work, neighbours would come to the house to watch but I think for all of us it was a bit strange; almost magical.

Granny refused to watch television at all, claiming it was downright evil. I think she knew that the arrival of both electricity and television in the village heralded great change in the way the family and the community had lived for so many generations. Granny didn't like change and she wasn't exactly a modern thinker. Granny was set not only in *her* ways, but also in the ways of her grandmother, great grandmother and back through many generations. For Granny, no matter how hard the life, following the traditional ways was still better than adopting radical new ones. To an extent, her misgivings were later justified. Modern amenities have brought great change to rural areas and the traditional village way of life, but not always for the better.

Before television arrived, the only real entertainment we had in the village was when the travelling movie show visited, every few months. That was very exciting for me and the other village children. A white sheet-like screen would be strung up in the grounds of the monastery and all the villagers—except a somewhat disapproving Granny—would gather and sit on bamboo mats on the dusty ground to watch an old Thai action movie. The shows were free but halfway through the movie would be stopped for about thirty minutes while the presenters got down to the real business of the evening, which was selling medicine.

At that time there was no pharmacy, clinic or hospital within a convenient distance of the village, so the movie shows were almost the only opportunity the villagers had to hear about or buy modern medicines. They were mostly just aspirin, stomach powders and the like, but they were presented almost as magical cure-alls. Five different brightly coloured pills were packed together in a small plastic bag and sold for a few baht per set but there was no information about what they were and no instructions as to what they were for, so those villagers who bought them usually took all five pills together, whatever their sickness. The salesmen had a hard time selling them, though. Apart from the fact that we had little money, many older villagers didn't trust the new medicines and wouldn't buy them, preferring instead the tried and tested traditional herbal remedies they could get free from Granny. Years later, the cure-all packs were banned from sale by the government as being useless and potentially harmful.

Granny refused to go to the movies because the sometimes violent images disturbed her too much, but she had difficulty understanding the soundtrack anyway. Granny didn't speak modern or Central Thai very well at all and instead spoke an ancient northern dialect called Khammueang, the language of the old Lanna Kingdom. Many of the older villagers, including Granny, referred to themselves as Lannathai, rather than Thai. All my conversations with Granny were in Khammueang. I'd been brought up speaking and hearing the dialect every day, though at school we were only allowed to speak Central Thai. (The teacher told us that if we ever left the village and spoke Khammueang, city folk would know we were country bumpkins.) Instead of a night out at the movies, Granny preferred to stay at home making bamboo baskets and traps, which was almost a hobby for her.

While weaving her baskets, Granny endlessly chewed a mix of areca nut parings, tobacco and lime wrapped in betel leaves, spitting the resulting blood-red juice into a tin pot. Betel is an evergreen vine and its leaves have long been known for their medicinal purposes, as well as for being a mild but addictive stimulant. The areca nut is the fruit of a species of palm tree and is also a mild stimulant. The betel leaf is smeared with mineral slaked lime and then the nut parings are added; in rural areas, tobacco is sometimes mixed in as well. The leaf is then usually rolled into a tight cone and chewed, though Granny popped each ingredient into her mouth separately. The blood-red juice that is spat out during chewing is caused by oils from the areca nut.

Chewing betel leaves with areca nut and lime is an ancient tradition in Southeast Asia and is mentioned on a thirteenth-century stone carving, believed to be the earliest known example of modern written Thai. An ancient saying in Thailand during financially difficult times is that 'rice is hard to find, betel is expensive'.

Preparation of the betel mix was a real art and most women in the village kept their ingredients in special bamboo baskets, which they carried everywhere with them, much as Western women carry handbags. Sharing one's betel with neighbours or guests was considered a very friendly gesture. In the early evening, when they had finished working in the paddy fields, a group of five or six elderly women would usually gather in the space under

Granny's house, exchanging local gossip while they went through the intricate ritual of preparing their betel. Chewing the betel mix is mildly addictive and stains the lips bright red, but Granny believed it helped preserve and strengthen her teeth. I'm not so sure about that, since she had hardly any left at all. Between chewing betel, Granny sometimes smoked a homemade cheroot made from locally grown wild tobacco, wrapped in squares of dried banana leaves. The cheroots had a rather bitter taste so at the same time she chewed a herbal leaf, which made the tobacco taste sweeter. Although Granny wouldn't let me smoke a cheroot, sometimes after chewing the leaf for a while she would take it out of her mouth and pop it into mine, so I could have a taste of the tobacco.

Because Granny was so involved with my daily upbringing, I think she felt she had a duty to pass on some of her knowledge to her grandson; to explain about our rural way of life, our traditions and superstitions, and why things were done in certain ways. When we sat chatting together in the evenings, she would usually impart some local folklore, story or tradition that she thought was important or useful to me. Granny was a great storyteller. Some of the stories she passed on to me had been told to her by *her* grandmother, so they were ancient tales. Granny's stories about the Rice Mother, monster snakes, forest pygmies and even a local Bigfoot fascinated me. I especially liked her ghost stories, though they often kept me awake for nights on end. Thai ghosts are very scary! Granny was an enthusiastic teacher and I was an eager student, but there were a few subjects she wouldn't talk about.

Although in our long conversations Granny might obliquely refer to the mating habits of the animals that lived in forest and field, she would never relate that to people. Sex-talk in the village was absolutely taboo and so was premarital sex. Visitors to some parts of Thailand, especially to the seedier coastal resorts, could easily get the impression that we Thais are very relaxed about sex, or even degenerate, but it's simply not true. Ordinary village folk were, and to a lesser degree still are, very shy about sexual matters. It was considered a private activity, not to be discussed. We boys certainly didn't have man-to-man chats about the birds and the bees with our fathers or even smutty conversations with our older male friends. Even the young men didn't talk about sex and probably didn't know much about it, though I wouldn't be surprised if some of the village girls had a quiet chat with Granny just before they were married.

Youngsters in the village certainly weren't promiscuous and I doubt if any of them were even sexually active before marriage. Our community was so small that everybody knew everybody else and many families were related in some way. It was difficult to get out of the village to look for a potential partner further afield and within the community there wasn't a wide choice of casual or even permanent partners, so there was really no opportunity for promiscuity at all. If there was, I think Granny would quickly have heard about it—and just as quickly put a stop to it. Granny was a stickler for propriety and maintaining village standards, customs and morals. If she heard about any premarital sex going on, a quiet word with the young man's father would have led to a quick marriage ceremony. Courtship in the village was slow and careful and I think for most couples the first night of married life was also their first sexual experience of any kind. I'm sure it was the same for my parents.

My mother was born in 1954 and was the fifth of Granny's

eight children. Her early life almost exactly reflected that of her own mother. Although my mother had three years of primary schooling, which was by then compulsory, she was still almost illiterate. She started working in the rice paddies when she was ten years old and married a local man with a background similar to her own when she was twenty, exactly as her mother had done. There was one major difference, though. Through many generations, the family members had no great personal ambition at all except to survive from day to day, but my mother was driven in almost everything she did by a determination that her only child would have a better life. If it hadn't been for that determination, I would probably have continued my family's long cycle of poverty, semi-literacy and apathy. My mother knew that the only way for me to break out of that cycle was to gain a proper education.

Things had improved since my mother's young days but even when I was a child only six years of primary education were free. For impoverished families, that still required what seemed considerable expenditure for uniform, books and classroom tools. Just as importantly, the loss of a pair of helping hands from the paddy fields, or the loss of cash income earned by labouring in the city, had to be seriously considered. However, because it was free, my father agreed that I could at least start my primary education. Unfortunately the extra costs soon proved too great and he later decided I would have to leave primary school after the third year to help in the fields, or get a job. I was very disappointed, though of course I never said so. What neither I nor my father had reckoned on was my mother's determination that I would study.

Granny didn't always approve of my father very much, probably because of his excessive drinking. She would sometimes take whatever was the opposite view to his, simply to be cantankerous. (I'm sure my father must have thought she was a dreadful mother-in-law.) I don't think Granny really believed that education beyond the most basic level was important for a future farmer like me, but if my father was dead set against it, she was all for it. With Granny's enthusiastic backing, my mother refused to allow me to leave primary school at the end of the third year. She nagged at my father for many months, trying to persuade him to find a job which would provide a regular cash income, even if it meant going to Bangkok to get it. Poor Father, he genuinely couldn't see the point of having to work harder just so I could be uselessly and expensively educated. He refused to listen to my mother's pleadings and demands or Granny's threats and muttered curses. He eventually upped and left us, though I don't think that was entirely due to the nagging. I believe he was simply unable to cope with the family's constant and unrelenting poverty and the exhausting work in the paddy fields. I later learned that my father did eventually go to work as a labourer in the city, but we never heard from him again. So that left just Granny, Mother and me at home.

Although I was only halfway through my six years of primary school, I enjoyed studying so much that I was already beginning to dream that I could finish primary and then continue to junior high school. I particularly enjoyed learning the Thai language and even at that young age I had the silly idea that I wanted to be a school teacher, rather than a rice farmer. Although I dreamed about going to high school, I knew realistically that it was impossible for someone from my background to study to such a giddy level. Nobody from any branch of my family had ever studied at high school. Despite my mother's enthusiasm, I knew we simply didn't have the money and, anyway, I was needed to contribute to the family income, especially since we were so short-handed after my father left. That meant leaving school after, at most, six years of primary studies, then working in the fields or labouring on a Bangkok building site. I put my dreams aside and accepted that my future would be the same as that of my parents, grandparents and so on back through countless generations: working for the rest of my life in the paddy fields, getting married to a local village girl and bringing up our children in ignorance and poverty.

The years after my father left were very difficult for Granny, Mother and me, though we were never hungry. I continued studying at primary school while my mother and Granny worked so hard every day (just the two of them now) trying to make ends meet and to cover my school expenses, as well as the small everyday family costs. Both of them laboured for cash in neighbours' fields, as well as taking care of our own paddies. They must have been exhausted but they never complained. I also had a difficult time. My school friends all came from large families with many children who could help with the chores or in the fields, but in my family there was only me and I had to work as hard as any adult. When there was no school, I also laboured in the neighbours' fields for just two or three baht a day, or I worked in our own rice paddies. On school days, I had to run home to carry more than ten heavy buckets of water from the village well to refill our storage jars, so that Mother and Granny could shower when they returned from the fields. I cleaned the house, foraged for food and fuel, cooked the meals and had a dozen other chores. I had no complaint about any of that, but I was only about eight years old and already my future seemed bleak.

Because my mother was so determined that I would finish primary school and continue to junior high school, she decided that she would go to Samut Sakhon, near Bangkok, to work on a building site. I knew she was very reluctant to go but we had to have a cash income and her determination for me to succeed overrode her fear of the big city. Granny simply accepted Mother's decision. To Granny, working in the city had always been the traditional and acceptable solution to financial problems. My mother knew I would be well cared for by Granny so she wasn't at all worried about leaving me behind. She went to Samut Sakhon and worked hard on the building site, mostly mixing cement, and doing as much overtime as possible. She not only had to support herself but also had to send sufficient money home for Granny and me. She was usually able to send about 200 baht each month and it had to be sent through the post in an envelope as cash, since there wasn't a post office nearby where we could exchange a postal order. Sometimes the money disappeared in the postal system before it reached us, which left Granny and me in great difficulties.

With Mother away, Granny becoming increasingly frail and me at primary school most days, our rice paddies usually had to be left untended. Granny's children helped out when they could be spared from their own fields and I also did as much as I could, but I started to regret ever having told my mother of my dream of studying. I began to feel that *I* should be the one working on the building site. It was an unhappy period in all our lives. I didn't know at the time that Mother was becoming increasingly unwell in the city, but she never sought medical advice. She didn't want to spend any money unnecessarily and just put her weakness down to tiredness caused by the hard manual labour and long hours. I rarely saw her during that three-year period because she was able to return to the village for only three days each year, during the Songkran New Year holiday. I missed her greatly but because of the money she sent home, I was able to continue my primary school studies until the sixth year and I then enrolled at a local high school, though I was never to actually study there.

During the years my mother was away, Granny had even more of an influence on me than before. I still needed the authority of a mother-figure in my life, so Granny and I became very close. I had lost my childhood awe and fear of her by that time and had grown to love and respect her very much. In her simple and down-to-earth way, she started to instruct me in the basics of the Buddha's teaching and I often accompanied her to the local monastery to listen to sermons. Although I was still young, Granny also decided it was time to instruct me in some of the more serious and arcane aspects of folklore and frequently talked to me about death and what might come after. In retrospect, I think she was actually talking to herself as much as to me and intuitively knew that her own time was not far off.

Granny died in 1991, aged seventy. Her death was followed two years later by that of my mother, who was thirty-nine. Mother died in Samut Sakhon just a month or so before I was due to start my high school studies. Both she and Granny probably died from diabetes-related illnesses, but nobody in the family ever knew for sure. Granny had been getting increasingly sick for several years. We didn't really know what was wrong with her but in those days there was no easy way to get her to the provincial hospital, so she never saw a doctor. She didn't trust them much anyway and preferred to rely on traditional herbal remedies which she made herself. Some definitely worked, at least in alleviating her aches and pains for a while.

Because I was so young, losing the two people I loved and

relied on most in the world within such a short period should have had a traumatic effect on me. I was naturally very upset but by that time I had learned so much from Granny about death—or at least the pragmatic Thai way of thinking of it—that I was able to accept the fact almost calmly. After they were cremated, their ashes were buried beneath a revered old pho tree in the monastery grounds. The pho or bodhi tree (*Ficus religiosa*) is the type of fig tree under which Siddhattha Gotama was meditating when he became the Buddha (*the Fully Awakened One*). Almost every monastery in Thailand has at least one very old pho tree in its grounds, often wrapped in yellow monks' robes. If a bereaved family cannot afford to inter a deceased loved ones' remains in a proper chedi in the monastery grounds, they may bury them beneath the pho tree instead, often in a small chedi-shaped tin container.

After Granny and Mother died an uncle tried to support me, but he had a large family of his own and couldn't afford to send his own children to school. He was also a traditionalist who, like my father, believed that education was unnecessary for a future rice farmer. It would have been easy for me to accept my fate; to give up my idea of studying and my dream to be a teacher, to live with my uncle's family and to carry on working in the paddy fields for the rest of my life. But my mother had wanted me to study, which was what I wanted too. I decided to ordain as a novice monk so I could continue studying at a monastic secular high school, which was entirely free. Unfortunately at the time there were few such schools and I had to leave the village and move hundreds of kilometres away to another province to attend one. I ordained in my village monastery but stayed there only a week or two before leaving for the big city monastery, so far away. I had just turned thirteen years old. I was excited by the prospect of studying but I was very sad to say goodbye to my little village and to my friends and relatives there.

After finishing my six years of high school studies at the monastic school, I disrobed from the monkhood. I was then fortunate enough to be awarded a university scholarship to study for a Bachelor Degree, and later for a Masters.

I am now a teacher of Thai.

The Right Medicine

I was a very healthy little boy when I was growing up in the village. I suppose the combination of fresh air, natural foods without chemicals or additives and plenty of exercise working in the rice paddies all contributed. The only medical treatment I ever needed was from my own granny and on two occasions from a very scary lady named Granny Perng.

Granny Perng was the local shaman, though I prefer the word 'healer'. She'd inherited her skills from her mother, who got them from her mother, who no doubt got them from *her* mother. From what I've read, Granny Perng perfectly fitted the fairytale description of a European medieval witch. She was aged about seventy and was very small, stick-thin and had a crooked back. She was always dressed in a dusty, black cotton sarong and had a mass of tangled black hair, thickly streaked with white. The only things missing were a broomstick and pointy hat. Everybody in the village was scared of her—while at the same time wisely paying her every respect—but Granny Perng was the one we always turned to in times of serious sickness, especially when it might involve ghosts or spirits. My own granny was excellent at curing most common ailments, small wounds or fractures and knew everything there was to know about medicinal plants and herbs. Most of the villagers came to her for advice and treatment for their everyday medical problems but for more serious issues we had to send for the professional. Granny Perng didn't use or need a lot of newfangled diagnostic equipment; no stethoscope, thermometer or anything like that. She made do with a ball of sticky rice and a length of string or, in especially difficult cases, an egg.

My first experience of Granny Perng's ministrations came when I was about eight years old. I was involved in a road accident. We didn't have cars in my village, and in fact we didn't even have a road; I was walking along a buffalo track and was hit by a drunk on a wobbly bicycle. I wasn't physically hurt much but the accident was such a shock that my *khwan* took off in fright. Thai people believe that the centre of their being, their khwan (perhaps spirit or soul) resides in the top of the head—which is why Thai people never touch each other on the head. The khwan is easily frightened and may exit the body in extreme or traumatic circumstances, leaving it in an 'empty' state and with symptoms sometimes similar to coma. Immediately after the accident and for several days later, I was in a state of shock. I could walk around but I was like a zombie: the living dead. My granny knew instinctively that my khwan had left me but that was something even her most powerful and secret herbal remedies couldn't cure.

My mother was sent to fetch the healer but, as was the custom, she didn't say a word to Granny Perng about what had happened to me. Granny Perng arrived at our house, carrying her tatty, black cotton bag of mysterious potions and lotions, herbs and spices, and various implements for grinding and mixing them. She silently observed me for a few minutes lying on the floor in my zombie state and then told Granny to bring a small ball of tightly compressed sticky rice, which she suspended from a short length of sai sin string. Granny Perng held the suspended ball of rice above my body and quietly muttered a few indecipherable questions. The ball of rice moved slowly from side to side, backwards and forwards or in a circle, the direction seemingly depending on the question asked. To nobody's great surprise, Granny Perng then diagnosed that I had been hit by a bicycle. She gave the exact place and approximate time, and confirmed that my khwan had left me.

That was serious because my khwan could get lost and not find its way back to me, but luckily the treatment was straightforward and the prognosis good. My mother was instructed to bring a bowl of hot water, into which Granny Perng sprinkled various crushed seeds, dried herbs and ground-up roots, being very careful not to let anybody see exactly what they were or in what proportions. She chanted over the bowl while the mysterious mixture infused and I was then washed from head to toe with it. My mother was next instructed to prepare a plate of offerings, including betel leaf, areca nut and tobacco, and to take it with a small fishing net to the exact place where I had been hit by the bicycle. There she had to gently wave the fishing net backwards and forwards whilst loudly calling out: '*Come here, Sorasing's khwan, come home to his body*'. She was to do that several times then leave the plate of offerings under any large old tree, before carefully carrying the fishing net back to the house. Considering my mother was almost illiterate, she was actually quite a modern thinker and told me later that she felt very embarrassed about all this. But she did as instructed and returned home with the net. The net was then shaken gently over my body, accompanied by more chanting from the healer. Granny Perng received her usual fee of small golden satang coins totalling one baht and tottered off home. Next morning I was fully recovered and able to go to school.

My next session with Granny Perng came about a year later, when I was nine years old. Like all village children, I'd been told many times by my granny never to make any loud noise in the house or nearby because that could attract the interest of a wandering spirit or ghost. I often forget, like all little boys in the excitement of some game, which always led to a scolding from Granny. On the occasion of my second visit from Granny Perng, I'd been playing a noisy game with some young friends in a field. Quite suddenly I felt very nauseous and faint. I returned home but by the time I got there I'd developed a high fever and flu-like symptoms which left me weak and hardly able to stand. Normally Granny could successfully treat fevers with her own herbal brews, but that time she again instinctively knew that whatever was wrong with me was beyond her healing powers. She sent for Granny Perng.

As before, Granny Perng spent a few minutes simply looking at me and then told Granny to bring a freshly laid egg from the chicken coop. She stood the egg on its narrow end and muttered a few questions, then let go of it and watched closely as the egg rolled around. Not only did it simply roll from side to side, it also stood up on end and made other very strange un-egg-like movements before finally coming to rest. From that Granny Perng was able to diagnose that I had been possessed by a wandering spirit, though one that was neither very strong nor particularly malicious. Again she prepared an infusion of water and herbs, but before I was washed with it she tied a length of sai sin string around my head. I was then washed with the herbal water while she muttered a charm over my body. A pause for a bit more muttering and I was washed a second time. Within hours my fever and other symptoms had completely disappeared. Granny Perng again received her one-baht fee.

There was a very odd aspect to that occasion which I didn't recall until many years after I had left the village. I was talking with some elderly village ladies about herbal medicines and happened to mention the egg diagnosis. I then remembered that after I had been washed the second time with the herbal water, Granny Perng told me to crack open and eat the raw egg that she'd used. I cracked it open—it was cooked. Until recently I thought I might have imagined that but I've since been told many times by elderly folk in several different regions of the country that the egg *always* cooks itself when used in treatment of this kind. That is so strange.

My co-author had his own experience of a village healer when he was the monk, Phra Peter Pannapadipo, and living in a remote rural monastery. In his book, *Phra Farang: An English Monk in Thailand*, Peter wrote that he started to develop an ache around his chest and under his arms. After a few days, the area became covered with small red lumps. They were neither painful nor itchy but seemed to be hot. He thought he might have herpes zoster (shingles). He told Yom My, one of the villagers, in the hope that he would arrange for him to be taken to the city hospital for treatment. In *Phra Farang* Peter wrote: 'Instead, Yom My called in the local healer; a very old man carrying a plastic shopping bag with a picture of Father Christmas on it.

'I had seen this old man in the village a few times but I hadn't realised he was the local shaman. Many Thai villages have these "doctors". They are usually very knowledgeable about animism, fortune-telling, folklore, massage and herbal medicines, but I had never seen one work before. They are frequently highly respected and consulted on all sorts of matters, not just medical problems.

'The doctor looked at my chest. Then he looked at Yom My. Some sort of understanding seemed to pass between them, as though to say, "It's hopeless, but we'll try". Nobody spoke. The doctor rummaged in his plastic bag, probably for his stethoscope, I thought. Instead he pulled out a very straight, very prickly, twelve-inch-long cactus. "*Yar*", said Yom My solemnly. *Medicine*. And what, I enquired nervously, was I supposed to do with it? "Boil it", said Yom My. That was a relief. And then I was to drink the liquid, I supposed. "No, no", said Yom My, as though he had never heard anything so ridiculous in his life. I was to pound the boiled cactus into a poultice and smear it on the lumps. But first the doctor would give me the main treatment.

'The doctor made three rheumatic but very respectable bows and then held my right arm straight up. He started mumbling a chant. I couldn't recognise the language but it wasn't Thai, Lao, or Pali. Perhaps it was a combination of all three, but it had a definite rhythm and he certainly wasn't making it up as he went along. This was a deadly serious charm he was weaving and his old face was screwed up in concentration.

'After a few minutes of chanting, the charm had been cast and then, much to my surprise, he suddenly blew into my armpit. I nearly burst out laughing but I thought that would be entirely inappropriate, so I kept my face as serious as possible. Yom My heaved a sigh of relief. I thanked the doctor who, apart from the chanting, hadn't said a word. He bowed again and Yom My helped him back to the village. Over the next few hours a stream of villagers came to wish me well, wish me goodbye or blow in my armpit. I wasn't sure if a monk should let ladies do anything quite so intimate but they seemed to think it was respectable so I let them get on with it. Within a few days, the lumps and aching had entirely disappeared.'

It would be understandable if readers dismissed all this as hocus-pocus. In my case, apart from the herbal wash, neither of my two treatments from Granny Perng actually involved medicine in any ordinary sense. But the fact remains that I was sick and after the treatment I got better. So did Peter. Of course, unlike Peter, I'd been brought up with a firm belief in ghosts and spirits and the tricks they can get up to, so I'm quite sure that my belief in them, combined with my equally conditioned belief in the healer to exorcise them, was as much a part of the cure as the herbal wash. Perhaps more so. Neither of my two problems seemed to stem from any obvious physical illness nor had obvious physical symptoms; both were caused by a spiritual imbalance of some kind, so perhaps I didn't need to ingest a medicine.

When a physical illness with known and obvious symptoms was present, village healers, including my granny, did prepare sometimes very complicated and secret decoctions, infusions, tinctures and salves from herbs, roots, plant stems, leaves, flowers, minerals and other natural ingredients, even including crushed insects. They were often very effective in their own right as medicines but there was always a spiritual element involved too. Amongst simple rural folk just a few generations ago, almost *every* illness involved a spirit or ghost of some kind, so to those folk it made as much sense to appease or exorcise the spirit as it did to drink or apply the medicine. Appeasement or exorcism of spirits or ghosts wasn't restricted to medical problems. Even now in modern Thailand, building a new house, planting a new field or buying a new vehicle usually involves chants, rituals and offerings to various spirits.

I would very much have liked to have talked to Granny Perng about her skills but she died long ago. I probably wouldn't have learned much from her anyway. All healers are very secretive and rarely share their arcane knowledge with anybody outside of the craft. Even my own granny didn't like to talk about her herbal medicines very much. Details of treatments are rarely written down and instead are passed orally from teacher to student, through the generations. If there's even a one-generation gap, the knowledge may be lost forever. I do know that before the new healer can begin to use his or her skills, a lifetime vow must first be made to a guiding spirit. Devotion to the spirit and to the craft must be shown by permanently giving something up; that could be sex, or a particular food, alcohol or even just a vow never to use particular but ordinary, everyday words. If the healer forgets or ignores the vow, the healing power is likely to disappear or, sometimes, to rebound with very unpleasant results. I have also been told that an established healer doesn't choose the person to whom the secrets are passed on to. The would-be apprentice must approach the healer and request to be taught the ancient skills.

In some village communities there were and still are three types of healer; one specialising in herbal remedies: *Mo Ya* (Medicine Doctor), one specialising in ritual, charms and incantations: *Mo Phi* (Ghost Doctor) and one specialising in wounds and broken bones: *Mo Kraduk* (Bone Doctor, also sometimes called Bone Blower). The specialities often crossed over. The Bone Blower not only repaired broken bones and healed wounds using splints, poultices and salves but also blew chants and incantations onto the affected area. Sometimes, as with Granny Perng, one healer might combine aspects of all three disciplines, though Granny Perng's speciality was as a Mo Phi. My own granny's speciality was as a Mo Ya, though preparing and applying her herbal remedies always also involved incantations and charms. Whatever their speciality, village healers rarely benefitted in a practical sense from using their skills and arcane knowledge, though they gained great prestige in the community. They were dedicated to their work and certainly weren't healing for money: they weren't charlatans. Most charged only a single baht or less and often gave their treatments free. I never once saw my granny charge any patient for treatment, though she was usually happy to accept a token gift of betel leaves, fruit, fish or something similar.

Sadly, the healers' great store of knowledge and wisdom is rapidly disappearing. Although Granny Perng had many children, most had moved away from the village to work as labourers in Bangkok and none were interested in learning the craft. After she died there was nobody left to carry on the Mo Phi tradition in the village. Since rural medical clinics are now widespread and more easily accessible, perhaps the Mo Phi's art is no longer necessary anyway, but *something* has been lost.

Although my own granny couldn't cope with anything as difficult as an absent khwan, she was very skilled not only as a Mo Ya but also at the Bone Blower's art, at least for simple things like small broken bones and severed fingers. When I was about nine years old, a friend and I were trying to carve a toy gun from a piece of wood, using a very sharp machete. Granny had seen what we were doing and warned that we were going to have an accident, but she was a great believer in children learning from their own mistakes so she let us get on with it. Minutes later, my friend almost totally severed one of his fingers with the machete; half of the finger was literally hanging on by only a thread of skin. We went screaming to Granny. She showed very little sympathy but immediately ground up various herbs, roots and leaves, then mixed them with water into a paste and applied the resulting ointment to both pieces of the severed finger. Mumbling a charm, she held the two pieces of finger together and bound them tightly with a cotton rag, using a sliver of bamboo to make a splint. The wound and bone healed quickly and my friend didn't lose the use of his finger, though Granny's eyesight wasn't too good and the finger was never quite straight again. I've seen Granny use the same preparation for a chicken with a broken leg and it was always applied with great affect to my boyhood cuts and grazes to knees and elbows. I've since tried store-bought Western salves for such minor injuries and can say without a doubt that Granny's traditional remedy was more effective.

Besides making tinctures, infusions and salves to be used and applied in the usual ways, Granny had another very traditional method of delivering the medicine—she would spit it at her patients. Spitting medicine was quite a common form of delivery because it was believed that the breath of some healers was itself a form of medicine. (Old Thai Buddhist monks still sometimes blow on the heads of sick people, especially babies.) I once picked up an eye infection and despite bathing my eyes frequently, the infection persisted for a week or more and gradually got worse. I asked Granny to cure it for me. She'd just been chewing her usual mix of betel, areca nut and lime. She spat out most of the blood-red juice, swilled some water around in her mouth and then sprayed the now pinkish water straight from her mouth and into my eyes. It stung for a few minutes but within a day or so the infection had completely cleared up. Another time when I had a different type of eye infection, Granny treated it with a few drops of warm breast milk from a neighbour who was nursing a new baby.

Spitting medicine not only worked on people. Granny was well known in the village as a skilled vet and she sometimes delivered the medicine to the animal via her mouth. A friend of mine was hunting with his dog in the forest when the dog disturbed a two-metre-long spitting cobra. These snakes are very dangerous. Not only do they have a venomous bite, they can also spit venom at their prey before attacking with their fangs. They can spit more than two metres, always aim for the eyes and are very accurate (just like Granny). My friend's dog howled in pain when the snake's venom struck its eyes and hastily backed off. The snake slithered away. Although the dog would probably not have died from the venom, it would certainly have been blinded for life. My friend was very fond of this particular dog so he took it to Granny to see if she could help. Granny took a lump of rock salt, chewed it in her mouth for a while, mumbled a charm and then spit the liquid into the dog's eyes. The dog recovered very quickly and didn't go blind. I saw her use exactly the same treatment for a young buffalo with an eye infection, which also cleared up very quickly. Rice whisky was also sometimes sprayed into the eyes for this sort of infection.

Many of Granny's herbal medicines acted in the same way as modern pharmaceuticals. Some took effect quickly (like taking an aspirin to relieve a headache) while others had to build up in the body over a period of time before they had the desired effect, like modern antibiotics. But they were all made for specific problems and to very precise recipes. It was never a case of grabbing the nearest bunch of mixed herbs, chopping them up and boiling them in a pot. Some ingredients had to be collected only during certain seasons, or at specific times of the day, from certain types of soil or during particular phases of the moon; a full moon was always best. Some flowers, herbs, plants and roots had to be freshly gathered and used immediately in their natural state, while others had to be dried, ground, infused or macerated. Animal parts, such as snake gall bladder or liver were sometimes added to the mix, as were minerals like potassium nitrate and camphor crystals. Some medicines were mixed or infused with ordinary water and others only with water that had previously been used to wash rice. Alcohol, lime juice or some other liquid might also be added.

The preparation of these medicines was a genuine and precise pharmaceutical skill and all stages of the preparation would include chanting, incantation and ritual. Granny was quite secretive about her herbal medicines and wouldn't usually let anybody touch any herb or plant which she had collected herself. If I went with her to the forest to collect ingredients, I could point them out to her but she wouldn't let me dig them up or pick them myself—only she could do that. Granny didn't want me touching her herbs because they had to be collected under very particular conditions while she chanted mantras and performed arcane rituals. She told me that if anybody except her touched them, their healing power could be reduced. She stored many dried herbs on top of the supporting beams beneath her house, kept in small airtight clay pots, wrapped tightly in cotton bags or hanging in bunches from the rafters. They were hung high so as to be out of my reach, partly because some of them were poisonous unless taken in very small and precise doses. Most villagers in Granny's day knew how to make a few basic herbal medicines-(some still do) but Granny was the only healer in the village and for kilometres around who knew all the secrets. In my village, they've mostly been lost since she died.

Some of Granny's potions were really quite pleasant to drink, you could almost feel them doing you good, and others had a disgusting taste. But not as disgusting, I think, as some traditional remedies I know of that were used at the time and still are used in the northeastern region of the country.

When I was at university I studied with a friend who grew up in a little village similar to my own, but in Sisaket Province in the northeast of the country. He was born in the same year as me and left his village to become a novice monk when he was thirteen years old, just as I did. As a little boy he frequently suffered from stomach upsets and his mother always prescribed the traditional local remedy—a live lizard.

Even visitors who have only been in Thailand for five minutes will have seen the friendly little *jing-jok* hanging upside down on ceilings and walls everywhere. The ten-centimetre-long bug-eyed gecko is totally harmless and very welcome in the house because it eats mosquitoes. But in the northeast, it's also useful as an immediately available, free and apparently very effective cure for stomach upsets. To take the medicine, hold the wriggling jing-jok by its tail, open wide and drop it down the throat, following up immediately with a drink of water to help the unfortunate creature on its way. According to my friend, that isn't as horrible as it sounds. Although the jing-jok may be difficult to swallow and can be felt moving around for a while in the stomach, it's soon killed by gastric juices and then quickly becomes effective as a cure. In the northeast, swallowing a live jing-jok is also considered beneficial for women immediately after childbirth, though as a midwife Granny never used it in her own postnatal treatments.

The jing-jok has other medicinal uses too. My friend told me he went through a period of bed-wetting when he was four or five years old. Eating the little lizard was the traditional remedy. To cure bed-wetting the jing-jok was cut in half, lightly fried and then swallowed without chewing. My friend took the medicine for about a month and his bed-wetting stopped.

The jing-jok's big cousin is the *tukkae*, so called because of the sound it makes: *too-kay! too-kay!* The tukkae grows to about thirty centimetres long and is a common food for rural folk throughout Thailand, usually chopped up and cooked in a curry (and very tasty it is too). If prepared in a slightly different way, it's also an excellent traditional medicine or tonic for malnourished toddlers. The tukkae has to be skinned, have its legs and half its tail removed, covered with salt, barbecued and eaten with sticky rice.

My friend told me of another common remedy which was used in his village to cure general aches and pains, rheumatism and colds. For those ailments a very large snail (probably the Giant African Snail) was rubbed bottom-down against a flat river rock. Although the snail quickly disappeared inside its shell, that was soon ground away until there was nothing to protect the creature. The pieces of shell were removed and then the gooey juice of the snail was mixed with water and drunk. According to my friend, that too was very effective.

Another traditional medicine in his village was a cure for toothache. In our childhood days, wild pigs were still common in rural areas. Besides being good to eat, the pigs' short tusks provided the main ingredient for several medicines in the northeastern region. For toothache, a little of a tusk would be ground against a river rock and the resulting powder mixed with water and various dried herbs and ground roots; galangal being an important ingredient. My friend drank such medicine several times when he was teething as a child and as a preteen and recalls that it gave almost immediate relief. That particular treatment was unknown in my province in the lower north, where for toothache we just used a mouthwash of salty water, but in my village the tusk of an old wild pig would often be worn on a string or chain around the neck, to both ward off evil and bring good luck to the wearer.

Like me, my friend grew up in a remote little village, far from any clinic or hospital, where local folk knew little or nothing about modern medicines. Even if they had known, health centres were almost inaccessible and treatment would anyway have been too expensive. To my friend, swallowing a live jing-jok or drinking snail juice was simply the everyday cure for everyday ailments, and he thought nothing of it. Now, with a university education, health insurance and living in a big city, he finds the idea as disgusting as you probably do.

Although Granny used only natural ingredients in all her medicines, happily they weren't usually *quite* as natural as to involve live lizards and puréed snails. Most of her medicines were made only from careful combinations of botanical materials and minerals. Whenever I had a cold or flu-like symptoms, Granny would make up an infusion of various herbs in hot water. She would cover my head with a cloth and I would spend half an hour or so breathing in the fumes. That was always immediately effective in clearing the head and nasal passages. Nose bleeds or sinus problems could also be stopped very quickly by chopping up and mixing dried mulberry leaves, camphor and garlic skin, wrapping them in a dried banana leaf and smoking the medicine like a cheroot, while blowing the smoke forcibly through the nostrils. Granny had similar simple herbal remedies for headaches, general aches and pains, stomach upsets, insect bites and minor wounds.[6] They all worked.

One of the most used herbs in Granny's arsenal was the rather smelly leaf of the little blumea plant, known in Thai as *nat*. She used it in various forms—mashed up, infused or smoked in a cheroot—and it was a cure for headache, nausea, low blood pressure, itchy skin, minor scratches and wounds and many other problems. She also used it in her postnatal midwifery treatments. Once, when I had a couple of nasty boils on my leg, Granny quickly cleared them up by applying crushed nat juice. The little leaf was also believed to be effective as a protection against ghosts because they didn't like the smell. At funerals in the village, older folk would twine a few leaves of nat in their hair or carry them in a pocket, so a ghost wouldn't follow them home from the crematorium. A very versatile and useful little plant!

Because rice cultivation is heavy work and involves a lot of bending, many older folk in the village suffered from backache and muscle strain almost every day of their lives. The obvious and traditional remedy is massage. Thailand is well known for its traditional massage techniques but the treatment must be given by a skilled and properly trained practitioner. Anybody can stretch limbs, grind joints or squeeze muscles but unless the practitioner knows exactly what he or she is doing, damage might be caused or an existing problem could be exacerbated.

Granny could give a simple massage but had never been trained in advanced techniques. She preferred not to do it, but there was little she didn't know about herbs. She often made up hot herbal compresses to use on her own aching body, or for neighbours. The compresses were very effective. She would take a square of thick, plain cotton cloth, about twice the size of a large handkerchief, and wrap up a quantity of various herbs and plants, including lemongrass, kaffir lime, turmeric and a root called *phlai*, which is similar to ginger. There might have been one or two more secret ingredients too. The package would then be twisted and tied at the top to make a soft, fat pad. Granny would dampen the pad and hold it for a while over the charcoal brazier, which would quickly warm the pad and release the healing properties of the herbs, as well as a wonderful aroma. The pad would then be pressed or rolled over the aching muscles, giving very quick relief from minor aches and pains. The same treatment was also effective for headaches, when the pad would be gently pressed onto the neck muscles. Once when I was accidentally hit just above the eye by a stone shot from a friend's catapult, Granny applied a hot herbal compress that alleviated the pain and reduced the swelling within minutes.

Granny was also the village midwife. Having given birth to eight children of her own, she knew all there was to know about traditional prenatal and postnatal care and especially about getting the new mother's body back into physical and spiritual balance after the birth. During the later stages of pregnancy, Granny's patients were allowed to eat only herbal soups and ivy gourd leaves and were forbidden to eat bamboo shoots, fermented foods or drink alcohol. For a short time after the birth only sticky rice and salt were eaten, but that was later supplemented with steamed fish, grilled chicken and bananas. For several weeks after the birth, the new mother was to go nowhere near any house cooking crab soup because the smell, although delicious, was very dangerous and could send her into a state of shock.

For a week after the birth, but for up to several weeks if

necessary, the new mother and her baby remained continuously in a specially prepared room, protected from the danger of evil spirits that might be attracted to the baby. Any gaps in the wooden walls of the room were filled with bamboo and other spiky plants, including sharp pineapple leaves, which ghosts and spirits cannot pass. Sai sin cotton was draped all around the room and pieces of cloth painted with magical symbols were hung from the corners.

Lying on a specially made bamboo platform covered in banana stems and leaves, the mother and her baby huddled close to a blazing stove fuelled with charcoal made from specific types of wood cut especially for the fire. The fire was kept burning continuously during the course of the postnatal treatment. Before the fire was lit, offerings of food, flowers and incense were made to the spirit of the fire.

Suspended over the fire was a metal pot full of boiling water and containing many different kinds of herbs, roots and minerals, kept constantly topped up. The room would be as hot and sweaty as a sauna. Besides breathing in the fumes, the new mother occasionally wiped her body down with the liquid and also drank as much of it as she could. Every midwife had her own formula for the herbs and other ingredients but Granny's included turmeric and nat leaf, though the key ingredient was a bulb from a sedge plant called *wan chak motluk*. The extreme heat, the herbal sauna, the fumes and drinking the liquid helped sterilise childbirth wounds and heal stitches, as well as getting the body back into balance. After a period of at least seven days, but sometimes longer, an offering of candles and flowers was made to the fire before it was ritually extinguished. This postnatal treatment, known as *Yu Fai* (staying by the fire), was common for new Thai mothers for centuries. (At one time, Yu Fai was incorrectly and negatively translated by missionaries as 'mother roasting'.)

With villagers' easier access to modern health care, through local clinics and health centres, the practice of Yu Fai had almost completely died out by the end of the twentieth century, except in the most remote areas. It is no longer practiced in my village, so Granny was probably one of the last of the traditional midwives.

At the beginning of the twentieth century, when Western medicines first started to become available in Thailand, the government tried to ban our own centuries-old traditional medicine, denouncing it as unscientific quackery. Things have changed in recent years and the government now actively promotes the use of many traditional medicines and treatments as a viable alternative to some imported, expensive Western drugs and treatment methods. They've even given their use a name: TTM (Thai Traditional Medicine) defined as 'the practice of the healing arts using knowledge gained from traditional texts or study, which is not based on science'. Modern TTM is an holistic approach to health and wellbeing and includes proper nutrition, physical exercise, the use of herbal medicines and therapeutic massage. Of course, it doesn't include diagnostics using sticky rice, string and freshly laid eggs, but there is still always a spiritual element involved, even if it's only to give thanks to the spirits and to the memory of previous teachers. Thai universities now even offer degree courses in TTM, ensuring that at least some of this valuable knowledge will be passed on to future generations.

There's no doubt that the value of TTM is now being recognised worldwide, not just by alternative or holistic treatment centres but also by some mainstream Western pharmaceutical companies. Many of the herbs, roots and other natural ingredients used in their basic and perhaps primitive form by my granny, Granny Perng and countless generations of village healers are now under intense and very serious scientific investigation. Some will undoubtedly make important contributions to world health and a few have already done so, even in the treatment of cancer. Although the traditional healing craft may have been largely lost at the local level, perhaps it will return in the future even to remote Thai villages in the form of better and more efficient medicines.

Snakes, Spiders
and Creepy-crawlies

Looking back, I realise that life in the village was full of dangers, especially for a child, though they were of a quite different kind to those found in the big cities. In the village we had no speeding traffic, no thieves, muggers, house breakers, murderers, rapists or 'stranger danger'. Our dangers were mostly natural but there were a lot of them and they were liable to drop out of a tree, jump out of a bush or come slithering or crawling along the ground at any moment, with their fangs, claws, stings and deadly venoms always at the ready. Snakes, huge spiders, giant centipedes, scorpions, blood-sucking leeches and vicious biting ants were all part of my childhood environment. But just as a city child would soon learn how to safely cross a busy road and to be aware of other urban hazards, so too did I learn early about the daily dangers in my village.

For the first thirteen years of my life I was surrounded by such creatures. They didn't usually bother me and I tried not to bother them, though confrontation was sometimes inevitable. Granny taught me from an early age that every creature, no matter how small, had its own place in the overall scheme of things, though she couldn't have understood or explained the scientific *why*. She had an almost symbiotic relationship with the creatures we regularly encountered and she taught me to develop the same attitude. She didn't love or hate these creatures in any sentimental sense but, with one strange exception, she didn't fear them either. She even seemed to have the uncanny ability to communicate on some level with certain animals, especially buffaloes. She appeared to have a very strange and special relationship with these gentle creatures, one that probably few ordinary farmers shared. I would sometimes see her in a paddy field talking to a lone, old buffalo, with her arm draped across the animal's neck, talking gently and quietly into its ear. Because I had lived with Granny all my life I didn't think that was particularly strange at the time; it was just Granny being Granny. She and I often walked together in the forest and she would point out the different trees and plants, animals and insects, explaining the nature and habits of each. Her own granny had done the same with her, when my granny was a little girl.

Small and sometimes not-so-small creatures were part of my environment but they were also part of my diet. Until I was about nine years old, there was no shop in the village where we could buy ready-prepared food, conveniently and anonymously slaughtered and prepackaged in polystyrene and plastic. We didn't have money for store-bought food anyway and had to eat what we could catch or grow. Because we were Buddhist we preferred not to take any life but if we wanted to eat meat or fish it was necessary to kill the animals ourselves—but we were never casual about killing.

Granny had a very sensible and balanced attitude towards the natural world. She always said that we should take what we needed from it, but nothing more. She also taught me that I should respect the right of every creature to live its life without suffering and that I shouldn't harm even the smallest of them except for food, or unless my own life was threatened. That attitude has always stayed with me. In the village we never captured any creature and kept it unhappily or unnecessarily penned up, to be used for food at some future time. The animals ran, swam or slithered free until needed (unlike in modern factory farming) and they were killed as quickly and as humanely as possible. A short prayer of thanks for the guardian spirit of the creature might also be offered.

Although we tried to live in harmony with all the creatures around us, snakes could sometimes be a problem. There are about 170 species of snake in Thailand. Most can give a painful bite and nearly a third are venomous: a few are deadly. I saw at least one snake every day of my life in the village and I mostly ignored them, being cautious only when I recognised one as being particularly dangerous, like a king cobra or krait. Granny had taught me to differentiate between the various species of snake and I was well-versed in snake-lore by the time I was about five years old, when I could put the local name to any snake that slithered across my path. Some snakes, especially king cobras, were dangerous but they were very good to eat and were also believed to have medicinal properties. Some other very large snakes had a spiritual significance and we tried never to kill them, even for food. If they were a threat to us we preferred, if possible, to catch them and release them unharmed into the forest.

Large snakes were regularly seen around the village but were most common during rice harvest time. The new rice would attract large numbers of rats to the paddy fields and the rats would attract the snakes. The village was surrounded on all sides by fields and forest, so there was always a huge population of snakes in the vicinity. Although Granny taught me to be very wary of snakes, she also taught me not to fear them. If I saw one and recognised it as being dangerous, I was to try and give it a wide berth. If I came unexpectedly on a dangerous one and it reared up at me, if I couldn't get away safely I was to stand my ground, showing no fear. Then, Granny said, even something as deadly as a king cobra might back down—but only *might*. If it didn't, and it spread its hood ready to strike, then I had no choice but to defend myself. No village boy was ever without his trusty catapult and I was a very accurate shot with mine. The fact that the snake was rearing with its hood spread out actually gave an easier target. Even a big snake could usually be scared off with a single well-aimed, homemade clay pellet or small stone. But you needed a strong nerve to face down a big king cobra. They can grow to about five metres long and when they rear up, a third of their body length is off the ground, so they could tower over a little boy like me. Happily, I never had a close encounter with one of the really big ones.

The closest I came to a big cobra was when I was about ten years old. Some friends and I were foraging in a field for food when we saw the tip of a snake's tail disappear into a hole in the earth, beneath a large abandoned termite mound. The snake was so quick that none of us were able to identify it, but we decided to try and catch it anyway. That was very foolish because we'd all been told by our mothers and grandmothers *never* to try to catch any snake unless we were absolutely sure what it was. I suppose, being in a gang, we all wanted to prove to each other what big brave boys we were, so we ignored the advice on that occasion.

The snake had disappeared into one of many rat holes. These holes join up underground, so the snake could have been anywhere. We blocked off all the holes except one with balls of grass, so the snake couldn't escape, then foolishly started to enlarge the remaining hole by pulling away the soft earth with our hands. One of my friends dug into the earth and was immediately and painfully bitten on the hand by what we belatedly recognised as a cobra. Despite some initial screaming and jumping up and down in shock, my friend had the sense and knowledge of snake-lore to keep as calm and as still as possible, with his hand not raised above the level of his heart. We quickly made a tourniquet from the rubber strap of a catapult, sat our friend on a bicycle and pushed it as fast as we could to a health centre which had opened just a few months before, only a few kilometres from the village. The health worker administered the anti-venom, as well as a telling off. Next day, the whole of one side of my friend's body was horribly inflamed and his arm was so tender and swollen it looked as though it might burst. But he survived. Granny scolded me for ignoring her advice and said it would have been a good lesson for me if *I* was the one who'd been bitten, but I'm sure she didn't mean that. The two-metre-long cobra was later caught under the termite mound by the bitten boy's big brother, and a very tasty curry it made too.

The largest snakes common to my village were reticulated pythons; the longest snakes in the world. They're not venomous but they are very aggressive and quickly bite if disturbed or frightened. They grow so big that it isn't unknown for them to swallow small children whole. I don't think that had ever happened in my village though Granny often told me that it *could*, just to make me more wary of the snake. But it was also true; I was a very small child and even a medium-sized python could quite easily have eaten me. Although its length is disputed,

I've read that a reticulated python of about twelve metres long was caught in Thailand. That's apparently a world record, but Granny believed they can grow much bigger.

Granny once told me a story that *her* grandmother told her, so this encounter would have happened more than a hundred years ago, before pythons were hunted so widely for their skins. Thailand's forests and jungles were much denser then and some were almost impenetrable and largely unexplored. When she was a young girl, Granny's granny went with several friends into the forest to collect bamboo shoots to eat. They stopped for a rest and sat down on what they thought in the forest gloom was a fallen tree trunk, partially covered with dirt and leaves. Within moments of the girls sitting down, the tree trunk started to slowly undulate. They jumped up in fright and realised that the tree trunk was actually a huge python. Although it sounds impossible, considering scientific records, Granny's granny thought the python was *at least* fifteen metres long, which I think would make it longer than any python ever recorded.[7]

The python didn't attack the girls because it had a great bulge in its stomach—which they had sat on—so it had obviously recently eaten something very large and was digesting its meal. Depending on the size of the prey, digestion can take several weeks and leaves the snake lethargic and almost unable to move. The girls ran for their lives, though they were actually in little danger from the already satiated monster. Being simple country folk, it's quite possible that they overestimated the length of the snake, but Granny thought the opposite might be true. If three or four people sat on a log it would have to be of a fairly substantial size to make a convenient seat, so Granny thought the snake might actually have been *bigger* than the girls' estimate. Granny also believed that such giants might still exist, deep in the jungles and forests or hidden away in deep, cool caves. If they do exist, I very much hope they don't end their days as shoes, belts or handbags.

Granny also told me of an encounter between my grandfather and a giant ten-metre-long python. He was hunting with his homemade black-powder musket in the forest and saw the snake hanging high up in a tree, with its coils wrapped around a small deer which was still feebly struggling. Apparently it's very unusual for a python to take its prey up into a tree before eating it. Granny told me that Grandfather said the snake had done something else very strange: it had inserted its tail quite deeply into the deer's rear-end, which he had never seen any snake do before. Normally a deer would have provided many excellent meals for my grandfather's family but to get the deer he would have had to kill the python. Granny said he would never consider doing that and, she told me, Grandfather understood that the snake needed to eat too, so he left it in peace. My grandfather felt he'd had a very narrow escape. Because the deer was still struggling, it had obviously been trapped only minutes before. If he had passed that spot earlier it could easily have been him up in the tree.

In my childhood days it wasn't at all unusual to see four-metre-long pythons in and around the village or in the fields, though we also occasionally saw bigger ones, up to about eight metres long. But even the smaller ones are dangerous because they are so strong and heavy. Once they get their coils around their prey, which they can do in seconds, it's almost impossible for the prey to escape. They don't actually crush their prey, as many people believe, but instead tightly constrict the chest and breathing until the prey suffocates. Pythons are most active after dusk and they would then sometimes slither silently into the village looking for something to eat. Chickens, ducks, cats and even large dogs would often disappear overnight. We had to be especially careful when walking about after dark because there were no street lights in the village and the houses had few lights inside and none outside at all. To go to the outhouse at night was always a nerve-wracking experience, not just because of snakes but also because of the many other dangerous creatures that might be around, or even lurking in the unlit outhouse itself.

However big or dangerous the python, we would never kill one if it could be avoided and pythons were never eaten in my village. The reason was that there are many large pythons which apparently have only one eye or, curiously, only one nostril. I never saw either, but that's what Granny told me. In my village, and in other parts of Thailand too, such animals were believed to be guardian spirits of the forest. To kill or harm one was considered particularly unlucky, but in the dark nobody was prepared to do a nostril check on a dangerous eight-metre-long snake, so we treated them all with equal respect.

If a python got into the house, or was seen nearby, the traditional method of catching it was to lasso the snake just behind its head. But there was no point trying to lasso it with an ordinary rope; it apparently just doesn't work and the animal continues to thrash around and be unmanageable. Granny told me that the lasso had to be a rope made from the fibrous skin of a banana tree. As soon as that was around the creature's head, or even just laid over its neck, the snake would become completely docile. The snake could then be grabbed just behind its head, put into a large covered basket and carried to the forest to be released. I've heard that the same type of fibrous rope is used for catching big pythons in villages in the northeastern region too, so the belief is obviously widespread.

My co-author had his own very close encounter with a python when he was a monk, living in a rural monastery in the lower northern region. A villager had caught a four-metre-long python and brought it to the monastery in a large stone water jar. Peter wrote that the snake had a cord tied around its neck and was very docile: so much so that he was able to put his hand into the jar and stroke the snake's head. The cord could have been made from banana fibre. Peter wrote that after a few days the snake escaped from the jar and was seen moving lethargically around the monastery, still with the cord around its neck. It finally took up residence directly underneath Peter's hut in the forest, where it lay quietly and didn't move for several days. Peter eventually dragged the heavy creature out from beneath his hut and sat with the snake's huge head in his lap, while he gently cut the cord away. (A very monk-ish but dangerous thing to do!) After a few hours the snake recovered its energy and slithered off into the forest, unharmed.

There's also the well known true story about one lady's unfortunate night-time experience with a python, though this didn't happen in my village. Happily, all the people involved survived. The lady was sitting in her unlit outhouse ruminating and put her foot on something soft. Wondering what it was, she reached down and touched it. It was the head of a medium-sized python. The snake immediately bit her hand and then swiftly wrapped its coils around the woman's entire body, pinning her to the toilet seat. Hearing her screams, a neighbour came running and tried to release her, but the snake bit right through the artery on his wrist. Another neighbour was eventually able to grab hold of the snake's head and drag the creature off. Rather than kill the snake, he decided to take it to the local town hall for officials to dispose of. Getting on his motorbike, he foolishly drove off with the snake draped over his shoulders. As he drove through the town, the snake suddenly coiled itself around his face and throat and tried to suffocate him. He crashed his motorbike and lay writhing around on the road, seriously injured and tightly wrapped in the snake's coils, while passers-by tried to rescue him. The snake eventually let go its grip and was subdued. Sadly, rather than being released back into the forest, the snake ended up in a zoo.

I had my own potentially fatal encounter with another type of dangerous snake when I was about eight years old. The rice store outside Granny's house was supported on stilts to protect the rice from rodents. The one-metre-high space beneath the store was enclosed with a lattice bamboo fence, making a coop for a few chickens which supplied us with eggs. The fence was there not only to keep the chickens in but also, theoretically, to keep big snakes out, since many snakes eat chickens. It was my duty to collect the eggs each morning. I crawled into the coop one morning on my hands and knees and felt something tap me sharply on the top of my head. I thought it was just a stick and brushed it away. It tapped again. Turning, I came face to face with a very venomous green pit viper, just a few centimetres away and preparing to strike at me again.

This particular snake only grows to about a metre long and the one enthusiastically trying to bite me was not fully grown, at about half size. That was just as well because, being a youngster, it only had a small jaw size and couldn't get a hold on my scalp. If its fangs had pierced my skin, I would have suffered a very painful and venomous bite which might easily have been fatal for a small child. Several adults had died in the village after being bitten by this type of viper, though its bite is not usually deadly if anti-venom is administered quickly enough. Anti-venoms for most snake bites were available in the city hospital but in those days there was no way to get a victim there quickly enough, so the bitten person usually died. When I was attacked, I grabbed a stick and was automatically tempted to beat the snake to death, but Granny had always taught me never to kill any creature maliciously or out of revenge because that would be bad *kamma*. I thought about her words just in time, and then simply chased the snake away.

Despite being dangerous when alive, many snakes were considered very good to eat and the king cobra especially was a delicacy in my village. Chopped up in a very spicy curry with black peppers, chilli and hot herbs, the snake was believed to boost energy levels generally and sexual energy specifically. Some people, including my aunt, seem to be allergic to king cobra curry. She told me that about an hour after the first and only time she ate it, her entire skin took on a scaly snake-like appearance. Her strange condition lasted nearly twenty-four hours but then disappeared without any after effects. The king cobra has a small gall bladder which is sometimes removed from the snake, put in a glass of rice whisky and swallowed, apparently with much the same effect as Viagra. (That was never admitted to by the village men, who claimed it simply gave them extra energy.) Women rarely drank it but it was, and still is, much favoured by men in rural areas.

In some regions of Thailand, the blood of a freshly killed cobra is believed to have medicinal properties and is sometimes drunk directly from the snake's body, immediately after its head has been cut off. Alternatively, the blood can be mixed with alcohol and left for a few weeks before being drunk. In the annual Thai–US military training exercise in Thailand (Cobra Gold) US troops are taught by Thai troops how to survive in the jungle, which includes catching and eating snakes and drinking the blood of a freshly caught cobra.

Catching small snakes to eat wasn't difficult for me. If I saw a fresh snake trail in the dust, I would stretch a one metre length of fishing net across the trail, suspended between two bamboo sticks pushed into the ground, like a tennis net. The snake would return along its trail and get entangled in the net, when it could be safely killed. I caught many snakes for the pot that way and also regularly caught them with a well-aimed shot from my catapult.

Granny often warned me about one particularly dangerous creature—the giant red centipede. In a way they are more dangerous than some snakes because they are so much smaller and not as easily seen. They can grow to about thirty centimetres long, though the ones I usually came across were only about half that size. But that's still big enough for a creature that can give a serious venomous bite which will cause excruciating pain. A bite from a big one can cause agony for several days and even a bite from one just a few centimetres long can cause severe pain lasting hours. I know: I was bitten several times when I was a child. The first time, I was sleeping on the floor in Granny's house and woke up when I felt something crawling on my face. I didn't know what it was and automatically tried to brush it away. The centipede bit me on the forehead. It was a tiny centipede but within a very short time I was in agony and my entire head was hot and throbbing, to the point where I thought it would split open. The pain lasted four or five hours, though was much relieved by one of Granny's herbal ointments. On another occasion when I was asleep a small centipede crawled under my blanket and bit me on the leg. I never saw the creature that time but I recognised its bite mark: two distinct puncture wounds. I still have the tiny scars, many years later.

The rainy season was the worst time for centipede bites because then the creatures would come into the house, looking for somewhere dry to spend the night. They would burrow under piles of clothes or blankets, or curl up in baskets, bags or in any convenient dark place. We had to be very cautious, especially as the house was so poorly lit. I never heard of anybody in my village dying from a centipede bite, but it would be possible if the person was allergic and unable to get treatment quickly enough. Although it's a very dangerous creature, the red centipede does have its uses. If a dead one is dropped into a bottle of rice whisky and left there for a week or so the drink becomes a strong tonic apparently giving extra energy.

In Thailand we have a huge and fearsome-looking spider called the black tarantula. I used to see them frequently when I was a child but I wasn't afraid of them. The spider has a very thick, solid body and its leg span can reach about fifteen centimetres. It looks as though it could easily kill but its venom is actually not much worse than that of a bee. We have hundreds of smaller spiders in Thailand, some of which are considerably more venomous than the tarantula. Although the tarantula is not exactly dangerous, it's extremely aggressive, fast to attack and can give a very painful bite. I was never bitten, but a friend of mine was while we were foraging in the forest one evening. A tarantula, mistaking his foot for passing prey, dashed out of its underground burrow, bit his ankle and dashed back in again, leaving him hopping around on one leg. Tarantulas usually eat cockroaches, crickets and similar small bugs, but a big spider can easily kill and eat a mouse.

Although tarantulas usually live in cool earth burrows, they're just as likely to be found in some dark, dry corner of the house, and especially amongst the logs in the fuel store. We often had tarantulas in Granny's house but they were welcome because they provided a quick snack; roasted for a few moments on the charcoal brazier and eaten like a crisp biscuit. They were a tasty treat for the village children and were also believed to be good medicine for toddlers who dribbled a lot. Granny showed me how to catch tarantulas when I was about four years old. Although they can move very fast, they're easily cornered and immobilised with a small stick, like a pencil, pushed firmly against the spider's head. The spider can then be safely picked up by the middle part of its body. In some parts of the country tarantulas are not considered good to eat at all. Local folklore records that eating the spider can turn the hair prematurely grey and may also lead to difficulties in walking, but I never heard that in my village.

Another common creature that looks as though it should be deadly, but isn't, is a huge black scorpion named the Asian forest scorpion. In the village it was known as the elephant scorpion on account of its size. I saw them often in the fields and forest, as well as sometimes in the house. They can grow up to about fifteen centimetres long and have a very painful sting but, like the tarantula's bite, the sting is only about as venomous as that of a bee. Smaller scorpions can be much more dangerous. Elephant scorpions live in underground holes, under rocks and in dead tree stumps and come out at night looking for bugs to eat. The elephant scorpion isn't particularly aggressive but will quickly attack if disturbed. Sometimes, if I lifted a piece of wood or a big stone in the forest, there might be a dozen of the huge creatures underneath, their stingers threateningly raised to ward off any danger I might present. I always avoided them if possible.

There were also dangers in the water. Whenever I told Granny I was going for a swim in the canal, she would always remind me: *keep your underpants on!* And good advice it was too. The canal was the home of blood-sucking leeches. They were unpleasant but weren't usually dangerous—at least not for little boys if they kept their underpants on—but they could attach themselves unnoticed to any soft skin and hang on until they'd gorged themselves on a couple of teaspoonfuls of blood, after which they dropped off. We had to be particularly careful about ducking our heads under the water because then a leech might swim into an ear, or even up a nostril. That could be very nasty because although they dropped off after feeding, their bodies became so engorged with blood that they would swell to four or five times their usual size, so they couldn't drop out of the nostril. Granny would have to burst the leech with a thin sliver of bamboo before it could be removed.

Although leeches are disgusting, for me and the other village children they were simply the routine cost of a hot afternoon spent splashing about in the water. When I climbed out of the canal there would usually be two or three leeches hanging from different parts of my body. They were easily removed by scraping a sharp knife down the affected body part. They could sometimes cause a mild infection but that was quite rare, though girls had to be more careful than boys. Leeches could enter the vagina, sometimes causing quite a bad internal infection, but one easily treated by Granny with a saltwater solution.

We also had to be quite cautious about leeches when drinking water. Our water came from storage jars or the village well and wasn't always very clear. If the sometimes cloudy water contained a small leech and it was accidentally swallowed, it could attach itself inside the body. I often collected a leafy plant that grew in the canal and that Granny used uncooked in a type of salad. Granny frequently warned me that the leaves had to very well-washed in case they had leech eggs attached to them. In that case, she said, the eggs could hatch inside the stomach, which is a very scary thought.

Although a swim in the canal usually meant giving blood to the leeches, it was also an opportunity to catch a huge edible water bug, *maeng da*, which looks similar to a cockroach but is about ten centimetres long. We had to be careful when trying to catch them because they can give a nasty nip, usually to the hand, but that was quickly and easily treated simply by urinating on the bite. Once caught, they were popped into an escape-proof bamboo basket, to be later lightly fried and eaten like a crispy snack, or mashed up and mixed with other ingredients into a curry. We children never went anywhere without a small lidded bamboo basket hung over our shoulders because we never knew when we might come across food.

My daily diet as a child usually included some small creature caught in field, forest or canal. It would have been difficult to find fresher food than I ate every day. It was often *so* fresh that it was still wriggling moments before going into the pot. Granny was a good cook, but she wasn't a chef. Cooking to her usually meant skinning and chopping up whatever creature I had caught a few hours before, adding freshly picked vegetables and various herbs and spices, stir-frying everything in an ancient iron wok and serving it up with rice. Sometimes the food would be barbecued, grilled or boiled as a soup. However it was cooked and whatever it was, our food contained no chemical colouring, no additives like monosodium glutamate and no chemical pesticide residue. I think few of Granny's dishes actually had names and she certainly would never ask me if I wanted *Tom Yam Kung* or some other particular well-known Thai food for dinner. Much of the world-famous Thai food that visitors to the country eat in restaurants or hotels was totally unknown to us in the village. Food was food and nothing more, cooked primarily for its availability and nutritional value, as much as for its taste. Despite that, it *was* delicious.

One of the most common little animals of my childhood were rats, though to me they were just curry-on-legs. Rats—or bandicoots rats as they are also known—were very much a part of my childhood diet, but we were fussy. Rats seen in or around the house were definitely not for eating. Because of their habits and possible food sources, they were considered dirty, unhealthy and inedible. The only rats we ate were those caught in the fields; they were plump from their diet of grain, clean in their habits and had a healthy, sleek appearance. At harvest time there were literally hundreds of them in the fields and we made every effort to catch them, not just to eat but also to protect the rice crop.

Granny made several different kinds of trap for catching rats. One was an ingenious little bamboo contraption that looked rather like a miniature guillotine. It had a bamboo hair trigger and when a rat passed through the trap and trod on the trigger, a thin piece of bamboo spring-loaded by catapult rubber would snap down on the rat's neck, breaking it instantly. In the evening, I would leave four or five traps in the rice paddies or near termite mounds and collect the rats in the morning. I could usually catch enough overnight to feed the entire family the next day. The traps didn't need baiting because the rats walked straight into them while foraging around in the paddies. The same traps were also good for catching small snakes.

When Granny was preparing rat, she first chopped off the feet and tail. We didn't eat those. She then made a long incision behind each of the rat's ears so the rat could be skinned in one quick motion, simply by holding the head and peeling the skin off the body. The head was then chopped off and wasn't eaten. The rat was sliced all the way open so the intestines could be removed, but the heart and liver were left inside. The rat was spread wide and barbecued over a charcoal grill. Instead of barbecuing, Granny sometimes chopped the rat up into very small pieces and mixed the meat with red chilli peppers, basil, garlic and other herbs, before frying with a little oil in a pan. The only oil Granny ever used was made from pig fat, which was the only cooking oil available to us in the village.

I know many Westerners think eating rats is disgusting, but they are actually very tasty and provide about the same level of nutrition as chicken or pork, but with less calories. Although I ate rats often as a child, I don't think I would like to eat them now as I'm sure they must be a less healthy food source these days, because of the modern chemical pesticides they ingest while foraging in the paddy fields. In my childhood days in the village, we didn't use chemical pesticides and the only fertilisers were natural. I suppose Thai people eating field rat is not much different from Westerners eating field rabbits. I've never tasted rabbit. There used to be many wild rabbits in Thailand but they're rarely seen anymore. I think we must have eaten them all.

Snake cooked as a curry or soup was another regularly eaten food, though not as often as I would have liked. Snake curry is absolutely delicious but catching large venomous snakes could be difficult, as well as dangerous, so a snake curry was something of a special treat. We ate many different kinds of snakes but king cobras of about two metres long were preferred.

Granny would first wrap the dead snake's head tightly in banana leaves to protect her hands from the fangs and venom. In some regions the skin is removed by using a sharp metal knife to slice open the snake down its entire length, and then peeling the skin off before cooking. Granny had a different method. The snake was grilled on a wood fire for a few minutes until its skin turned brown and crispy. She then cut off the head. That was discarded, but it couldn't just be thrown away. The head had to be buried quite deeply in the earth because it was believed that if somebody trod on it with bare feet, they could still be affected by the snake's venom. Granny would then use a sharp sliver of bamboo and run it quickly along the length of the snake, scouring the crisp skin away in long pieces. That exposed the white meat underneath. The snake was then sliced all the way down its length so the internal organs could be removed. If the meat was going to be fried, Granny would chop the snake into lengths of about twelve centimetres and put it in a pan with lots of very hot chillies, spices and a little oil. If it was to be made into a soup, it was chopped into shorter lengths and put into the pot with water, vegetables and herbs, but again with many very hot chillies and spices. However it was cooked, snake was a *very* hot and spicy meal and would always result in a lot of heavy sweating. Granny thought that was healthy. She believed that sweating not only cleared impurities from the body, but also stopped us getting fat.

Insects were another of my favourite foods, especially for breakfast or as a quick snack at any time of the day. Not only are they delicious, they also have a very high ratio of protein to carbohydrates and fat. I have read that kilo for kilo, insects contain more protein than fish or meat. We ate most insects crunchy fried: simply dropped into a pan with chilli and garlic and cooked in a little oil. My favourite insect dish was a little black beetle called *maeng-i-nun*. I could easily catch them at night when they came out from their underground burrows to eat foliage. By shining a torch onto the bush, dozens would come running into the light and could then be easily caught and dropped into an escape-proof bamboo basket, or a bucket of water. If they were big beetles, the wing casings had to be removed before cooking because they are quite hard and have sharp edges, but smaller ones could be eaten whole. Other insects which make a good meal and are cooked in the same way as maeng-i-nun include crickets, grasshoppers, locusts and wood worms. Bamboo worms are particularly delicious lightly and crisply fried, when they look very much like French fries. The giant water beetle is barbecued, as are Elephant Scorpions, while tarantulas are simply grilled until crispy.

All our food was delicious, nutritious and free. What more could anybody want?

It may seem something of a contradiction that rural people can appreciate and enjoy so much about their natural environment while at the same time seeing so many creatures as food. There was no contradiction for me as a child. Despite sometimes being very dangerous, the creatures around me were all beautiful and interesting. They were only viewed as breakfast, lunch or dinner when we needed something to eat.

Although I would often go foraging in the forest specifically for food, Granny and I also liked to walk there simply for pleasure and to observe the creatures around us. If we made any noise while walking, the little forest creatures would usually hide, fly away or remain very still until we had passed by. The forest would be totally silent, with not even the chirping of an insect. If we stopped our noisy progress and stood or sat perfectly still, after a few minutes the forest would come alive again and many creatures would reappear. Squirrels were amongst Granny's favourites. We have about a dozen different species in Thailand and they are all beautiful and amusing to watch, as they scamper through the tree branches. I would only kill one if I had been sent specifically to catch something to eat and couldn't find anything else. In the early evening, birds and bats were also fascinating to watch as they flittered silently between the trees. Bats could be a nuisance because they would eat the fruit from Granny's trees, so we had to protect the fruit by laying cotton netting over the branches. The net had the added advantage of entangling the bats, making them easy to catch. In the village, bat wings were considered a delicacy, after having been cut off and left to dry in the sun for a day or two, then fried in oil.

Birds, bats, squirrels, snakes, scorpions, spiders; all the little creatures seemed beautiful to me, except one, though even that was fascinating. The creature I was most bothered by as a child was also the smallest, but it was a daily nuisance. It would attack and viciously bite not just to defend itself, nor for food, but simply because it was so totally aggressive: the Red Weaver Ant. The ant grows to about ten millimetres, which is quite big for an ant, though it's not the largest found in Thailand.

Unlike some other ants, the red ant isn't venomous but to be bitten by just one is painful; to be bitten by an army of them is agony. Not only do they bite, they immediately follow up by spraying the wound inflicted by their fangs with formic acid squirted from their rear-end (Granny believed it was the ant's urine.) When they bite, they never let go. They seem to have just one response to everything they encounter: *attack!* One may simply drop off a tree, land on your head or arm and will immediately start biting.

As a child in the village, hardly a day went by without me being bitten at least once. I soon learned to shake out my clothes before putting them on, as well as checking my bedding before going to sleep (which was wise to do not only because of ants, but because of just about every other creepy-crawly thing too). Granny taught me to be especially cautious when walking in the forest or climbing a tree, because it was easy to brush up against a red ant nest, skillfully made of living leaves woven together and almost invisible amongst the other leaves. In a single tree there could be dozens of nests, inhabited by hundreds of thousands of ants. If any nest was disturbed, an army of soldier ants would immediately rush out to defend it, biting anything in their path. When they attacked, they would get into my hair, into my ears and eyes and inside my clothes, to the point where I would frantically tear my clothes off trying to escape from them.

Throughout Thailand, the Red Weaver Ant and its eggs are considered delicious to eat. They're usually eaten raw, mixed with a sour salad. Being so aggressive they can be difficult to catch in large enough numbers to make a decent meal, but Granny taught me a simple trick. We would place a large, tightly woven bamboo basket on the ground directly under the nest and then hit the nest with a bamboo pole. We had to be quick because in moments the soldier ants would be coming down the pole, ready to attack. After being hit the nest easily broke open and the ants and eggs fell into the basket. A basket doesn't sound as though it would hold a tree-climbing ant for a moment, but Granny taught me to powder the inside of the basket with rice flour. The ants couldn't get a grip on the powder and couldn't climb out of the basket. As a boy, whenever I wanted to climb a tree to pick fruit, I would cover my exposed skin with the rice flour, or sometimes with chalk powder. Even if ants attacked me, they couldn't get a grip on my skin to bite me. It really works!

Although the red ant was a big nuisance, it was also one of the cleverest little creatures that lived in my environment. Granny and I would sometimes sit for hours in the forest watching them build a new nest, though without getting too close. They seem to prefer the broad soft leaves of the mango tree but will build their nest in almost any tree or bush with suitably large, flexible leaves. To start to weave the leaves into a nest, the ants form several chains, gripping each other firmly in their mandibles, and the leading ants in each chain work as a team to draw two leaves together. Other members of the workforce then hold their own larvae between their mandibles and gently squeeze them until a silky thread is released, which the ants use to weave the leaves together. They work nonstop until they have a small and basic waterproof home, but then continue to expand the nest until it could be a half metre long and home to thousands of ants. I appreciated their truly remarkable organisation and skill, but I still didn't like them.

It's been many years since I lived in my village. I now live in a city, though even there in my garden I still sometimes meet some of the creatures I was familiar with as a child, including the occasional snake, giant centipede and, of course, red ants. I don't necessarily want such creatures near me anymore, and especially not inside the house, but I still very much respect their right to live and would never knowingly harm them. I don't eat them anymore because I don't need to. I sometimes see roasted tarantulas and bugs for sale on street stalls but by now I've gotten used to buying my food at supermarkets and find the idea of eating spiders and other 'exotic' food rather strange. But I'm very glad that I grew up in a rural environment and had the opportunity to get to see and understand some of these creatures in their natural surroundings, close up and alive. And I am grateful to Granny for having taught me so much about them.

I think Granny knew everything there was to know about the creatures that lived in and around the village, in the fields and in the forest. She knew their local names, their habitats and their habits. She viewed them in different ways; some had a spiritual significance, some were dangerous and to be avoided, others had medicinal uses and some were simply food. But she had no fear of any of them—except one.

The one exception was a little non-venomous creature that was hardly dangerous at all: the praying mantis. In Thailand, we have some large mantises; they do bite but they are almost harmless to humans, though they are deadly and vicious predators to their prey and to each other. Very strangely, if there was ever a mantis of any species or size in the house, Granny would become hysterical and rush outside, screaming for me to get rid of it. Granny was a strong-willed, sensible and calm woman and rarely showed emotion, so I have never understood her fear. She would never explain it to me, as though it was some dark secret unsuitable for a little boy to know about. In retrospect, I believe there must have been some important spiritual reason for her apparently irrational fear. I've since asked old folk in my village and other rural communities whether the mantis has some animist symbolism that Granny never told me about, but no one can give me an answer.

It remains a small and now unsolvable mystery about Granny's relationship to the natural world.

Ghosts, Ghouls
and Scary Monsters

We Thais are a very superstitious people. Even most well-educated Thais believe in ghosts of one kind or another—and we have a lot of ghosts in Thailand. Like Western ghosts, many of ours are simply the spirits of dead individuals who, for one reason or another, remain bound to the earth, perhaps lost or not even realising they are dead. It's widely believed in Thailand that the ghost or spirit of a deceased person will linger on close to the place where he or she died, at least until a ceremony is held by the family on the seventh day following the cremation, after which the spirit will usually move on to some other realm or to a new birth. In case it hasn't, additional ceremonies will be held on the fiftieth- and one hundredth day after the cremation. Even after that, daily offerings of food, water and incense may still be made to the spirit, sometimes for years. Granny made such offerings every day for the spirits of her own parents and grandparents. Many Thai ghosts or spirits seem to be harmless but some are malevolent, especially if they died suddenly and violently. Then they may stay longer to seek revenge on those who are still living.

We also have our fair share of generic ghosts, similar to some found in Western folklore, like ghouls, banshees, bogeymen and vampires, though in the Thai language they are all simply called 'ghost' (*phi*). Many of these are considered very dangerous and elaborate ceremonies may have to be carried out by a Ghost Doctor to exorcise them. There are also Thai ghosts that have developed over time to explain some unknown medical condition. One such ghost, *Phi Mae Mai*, seems very similar to the European succubus or 'Old Hag', which sits on the victim's chest at night and causes feelings of suffocation. There are also other ghosts that have grown out of Buddhist teaching stories. These ghosts are usually harmless and may appear to an individual to serve as a warning to that person. The majority of Thai ghosts seem to be female, and particularly malicious ones at that.

When talking with elderly village folk, I was able to identify ghosts from various regions of the country which had the same characteristics but different names. I also found ghosts with the same name but quite different characteristics. The name of a particular ghost can vary from province to province and even from one village to another, so it's sometimes difficult to precisely identify any particular ghost. Here, I've written about the ghosts that Granny told me about and which she particularly feared and which also seem to be found throughout Thailand. I've used their most common names, though they are not necessarily the names they were known by in my village.

The scariest ghost Granny told me about was *Phi Kra-Suea*. Her stories about this particular ghost kept me awake for many nights when I was a child, especially as the stories were usually told by the light of a guttering kerosene lamp, which cast spooky flickering shadows into the corners of the room. Scary, but thrilling too!

According to Granny, Phi Kra-Suea has the form of a woman, so beautiful and graceful that she can mesmerise anybody who looks at her. Although beautiful of face, her beauty literally ends there. Phi Kra-Suea has no lower body and instead has a mass of internal organs and bloody entrails hanging down below her neck, trailing along after her as she floats above the ground. Sometimes she disguises her lack of body by wearing a long flowing dress. Phi Kra-Suea is very dangerous and has a voracious appetite. Although she usually eats dead bodies and human excrement, she's also quite partial to weak living bodies, especially babies, and may even suck a baby from the womb of a woman during childbirth. As the village midwife, Granny always took precautions to ensure that Phi Kra-Suea was nowhere around before delivering a baby. Phi Kra-Suea often stays close to cemeteries where she has a ready supply of food, which is one reason why Thai people don't like to live anywhere near a cemetery.

I had my own scary close encounter with Phi Kra-Suea when I was about eight years old. Granny was caring for a neighbour's baby for a few weeks while the mother had to leave the village for some reason. The child was the only newborn baby in the village. Granny was very worried about this and knew the baby might attract Phi Kra-Suea, so she cut bamboo stems and other spiky plants and tied them around the stairs and all the entrances to the house, as well as stuffing them between the gaps in the wooden planks of the walls. With that protection, she said, nothing could get in. But late one night, soon after, the whole house suddenly began to shake violently, as though caught in an earthquake. I was terrified and huddled close to Granny, who clung tightly to me and the baby, while reciting charms and protective spells. The shaking was so violent I thought the house would collapse. I wanted to run outside but Granny said that would be even more dangerous than staying indoors. After a few minutes, the shaking stopped as suddenly as it had started. Phi Kra-Suea had given up. Next day, none of the neighbours reported any disturbance at all; whatever it was affected only our house.

Another very unpleasant and traditionally female ghost is *Phi Ka*, though she is known in the northeastern region as *Phi Pop* There are many different stories about Phi Ka, some of which give her contradictory characteristics, but all of them agree on one thing: Phi Ka is evil personified.

Phi Ka is often the ghost of an ancestor of its victims, sometimes possessing its own descendants or family members. The ghost likes to gnaw away at its victim's entrails—from the inside—and is said to particularly enjoy eating human liver. When Phi Ka possesses a human long-term, it can eventually turn that human into a cannibal who goes forth at night looking for fresh liver to eat, while the victim is still alive. Phi Ka so enjoys liver that it will cause the possessed person to loudly wail, demanding to be fed with its favourite dish.

Granny told me that symptoms of Phi Ka possession start with the victim speaking in a strange voice and behaving differently from usual. The victim's arms and legs may become very numb and he or she can simply fall over. Convulsions may follow and eventually the victim will enter a coma, during which the body can become completely rigid. If Phi Ka isn't exorcised by that point, or doesn't leave voluntarily, the victim will probably die.

If an exorcism is needed, the Ghost Doctor may perform a whirling dance around the victim, similar to that of the Whirling Dervishes of Turkey. As the dance reaches its climax, Phi Ka is sucked out and is carried away by the wind. People who claim to have seen Phi Ka being whisked away in this manner have described it as having a very thin, dark-skinned body, with a rotund belly and a huge mouth filled with very sharp teeth. Others have said it resembles a black dog, or a monkey.

Phi Ka doesn't always stay with its victim until he or she dies and may move quickly from one to another. If the current victim does die, Phi Ka may then possess another member of the same family: often a young female. Phi Ka sometimes stays only a very short time, even just a few hours, before moving on to a new victim. It can also possess large animals such as oxen and buffaloes, but they usually die within days of possession. In my village, the unexpected death of apparently healthy young buffaloes was usually put down to possession by Phi Ka.

Granny told me that a sure sign of the presence of Phi Ka was that an owl would be frequently seen on the roof of the house or perched nearby. A wandering Phi Ka looking for a new victim could appear as a horse, a white duck or a large black dog. It sounds very strange, but Granny also told me that a woman possessed by Phi Ka would have an invisible monkey sitting on each of her shoulders. Although invisible, the monkeys could be seen by looking through a small hole in a banana leaf, but if you could see the monkeys, they would know you were looking at them and would cause the possessed person to react violently towards you. I tried it once when I was a little boy. The woman I was secretly observing didn't have any monkeys on her shoulders but she saw me looking at her through the banana leaf. Knowing what that meant, she was absolutely furious with me and complained to Granny. I got a scolding for that.

Does Phi Ka a.k.a. Phi Pop really exist? Most educated people would say that of course it doesn't, but a Thai psychiatrist who researched cases of Phi Pop possession in the northeastern region came to a different conclusion. The psychiatrist, Dr Sa-ngun

Suwanlert, carried out his month-long study in 1967 amongst monks, government officials, psychiatric patients, spirit doctors and those who believed they had been possessed by Phi Pop. In his report he concluded: '*Phi Pop is not merely a legend, it is an actual occurrence*'.

Many Thai men are absolutely terrified—with good reason—of being visited by 'the widow'; a female ghost named *Phi Mae Mai* which has an insatiable sexual appetite. Although known throughout Thailand, including in my village, the ghost is particularly active in the northeast of the country and is most dangerous in the two or three months between the end of the rainy season and the beginning of the cool season. Phi Mae Mai seems similar to the European succubus, or 'Old Hag'. The ghost is constantly searching for a new mate and at night creeps into the bedroom of a sexually mature male while he is sleeping, suffocates him by sitting on his chest or stomach and then makes off with his spirit or soul. Victims often groan loudly in their sleep, just before they die. Not every Phi Mae Mai attack is successful. Some survivors have reported waking up in extreme fear and panic, their hearts beating unnaturally fast and with a feeling of being suffocated. Although Phi Mae Mai is invisible, survivors report that they could feel her presence in the room.

Some men, particularly in the northeastern region, are so scared of being attacked by Phi Mae Mai that even today they may go to great lengths to fool her. Some men paint their fingernails bright red at night and wear women's clothes to bed, so Phi Mae Mai will think they are female and leave them alone. In front of many houses can still be seen a very realistic-looking carved wooden penis, as much as a metre and a half tall, set there to distract Phi Mae Mai so she doesn't enter the house. I have even heard unsubstantiated stories of northeastern men who are so terrified of Phi Mae Mai that they have had their penis surgically removed, so the ghost won't be interested in them.

Although she's usually resident in Thailand, Phi Mae Mai seems to enjoy travelling abroad as well. Between 1982 and 1990, more than 200 apparently healthy Thai men died in their sleep from Phi Mae Mai symptoms while working as building labourers in Singapore. Some died in a similar way in Brunei and other parts of the Middle East. In recent years medical science has given a name to the strange phenomenon of healthy young men dying in their sleep: Sudden Unexpected Death Syndrome (SUDS), known in Thai as *Lai-Tai*. But whatever scientific name is given to it, the deaths are not really explained. For many rural Thai people, Phi Mae Mai continues to be the culprit.

Granny particularly feared a ghost named Phi Tai Hong, which is a very nasty, vengeful ghost with a violent grudge against the living. Phi Tai Hong can be either male or female and is the ghost of someone who died an unnatural, sudden or violent death, from murder, road accident and the like. It can also be the ghost of a baby who died soon after birth. The ghosts' untimely deaths make them want to seek revenge on the living by trying to possess new and healthy bodies. A ghost can sometimes be persuaded to leave its victim if enough offerings are made but if it doesn't it must be driven out by a Ghost Doctor, sometimes forcibly with a whip or bamboo cane.

One of Thailand's most common ghosts, though an apparently harmless one, is *Phi Pret*, the hungry ghost. The story of Phi Pret has developed from a Buddhist teaching story about what can happen after death to people who were greedy for material things in life, or too concerned with gaining wealth and power. Such a person risks being reborn as a Phi Pret, with a huge belly but a tiny mouth no bigger than the eye of a needle; always hungry but never able to satisfy its greed. Because they are always hungry, Phi Pret are usually bad-tempered and like to scare people, though I've never heard of anybody actually being harmed by one.

In his book *Little Angels*, about the lives of Thai novice monks, my co-author (then Phra Peter Pannapadipo) told the story about a personal encounter between a young novice and a Phi Pret. The thirteen-year-old novice broke the monastic rule by eating in the evening. Later that night he had to go to the bathroom, which was on the other side of the monastery grounds.

The novice said: 'It was very dark and I was just walking past an old tree when I suddenly felt sure someone or something was watching me. I was nearly stiff with fright, but I turned around very slowly. There was the ghost, standing behind the tree, staring at me with huge, round eyes. He was about twenty feet tall and had a very skinny body, except for his belly which was fat and round. He had long thin legs and arms that hung down to his knees. His hands had very long fingernails and his white hair was dirty and tangled, hanging over his shoulders and down his back. He didn't have any clothes on at all, not even a piece of rag to cover his *bug-hum*. He had a tiny mouth in the middle of a very ugly face. I knew what it was—it was a Pret! I knew the Pret had come for me because I'd been greedy and eaten rice in the evening. For a moment I couldn't move but then I screamed and ran, not looking behind me because I was sure he was chasing me for being a bad and greedy novice. After that terrible experience I decided I would leave that monastery and move to another one far away.'

Some Thai ghosts have very strange habits. *Phi Phong Khang* appears in the form of a skinny old black monkey and enjoys sucking the toes of people sleeping in the jungle or forest, though it doesn't usually bite and seems to be harmless. It's often found in forests close to salt flats, so perhaps it enjoys the taste of salty toes. An Englishman who knew nothing about Thai ghosts told me of his own encounter with Phi Phong Khang during his first visit to Thailand. He was staying alone in a resort on Kho Samui Island. The grounds of the resort contained many trees, rather like a forest, and was close to a beach and salty water; the sort of environment that Phi Phong Khang prefers. The hotel room was air-conditioned but that particular night wasn't hot, so the man left his balcony window open and slept under a mosquito net. He was very tall and his feet overhung the end of the bed, not quite covered by the net. During the night, he woke up suddenly when he felt a heavy weight hanging from his toes. He jumped screaming out of bed, thinking he was being attacked by a vampire bat but instead saw a thin, black monkey-like figure leap in one bound from the floor and through the open window. The man found no puncture marks on his toes but said they were wet and slimy, as though something had been sucking them.

In some regions Phi Phong Khang is known as *Phi Dut Lueat* and is more vampire-ish, sucking not only the toes but also the blood of its victim. If the ghost can be caught while in its monkey form, it is believed drinking its blood will give immortality.

Phi Ha is the ghost of somebody who died from cholera. There was a serious outbreak of the disease in Bangkok in the mid-nineteenth century, during which the ghost seems to have made its first appearance. There were so many dead that city monasteries couldn't cremate the corpses quickly enough, so they were disposed of by being thrown in the river or burnt without funeral rites. Phi Ha is a lonely, wandering ghost which is not usually dangerous but haunts the area where it died. Nowadays, when someone dies of a mysterious disease, Thai people may say that the person died of *Tai Ha*.

Phi Kra-Hang is a very odd and rare ghost found only in a few remote rural areas, though Granny told me it had been seen in our village. The ghost is male and is usually bare-chested but wears traditional northern-style pants. Strapped to its skinny arms are stiff wings made from the flat, circular bamboo trays that farmers use for sifting rice. It lives in farmyard barns and flies through the air at night sitting on large wooden rice mills, looking for excrement to eat. Although its appearance is frightening, the ghost seems to cause no harm.

Phi Phong is a male ghost found in the north of Thailand, living in a small white sedge plant called *waan*, which has a bad, acrid smell. Old plants may give off a glow at night—a sure sign that Phi Phong has taken up residence. The ghost has a glowing nose which drips sticky fluorescent snot, leaving a shiny trail on the earth. It leaves its plant each night to look for toads, frogs and fish, which it eats by noisily sucking out their juices. Although Phi Phong is quite shy and scared of people, it's generally beneficial and will protect the plant owner's home, especially from other less-welcome ghosts. But Phi Phong is easily upset. If a human hurts the ghost or its plant, it will get revenge by taking a wooden pole from a widow's house and throwing it over the roof of the victim's house. That will bring bad luck to the occupants and the house itself will collapse soon after. I've heard that if you meet Phi Phong, it will offer you gold if you promise not to tell anybody about its disgusting eating habits. Unfortunately, in the morning the gold will have turned to charcoal.

When I was a boy in my village, I often went with other boys to the rice fields at night to catch frogs to eat, using a phosphorous torch to light the way. One night, after collecting enough frogs, we returned to the village, where we realised one of our gang was missing. There are many dangers in the forest at night so we went searching for the boy and eventually found him kilometres away, totally confused and disorientated. He told us that while walking through the fields, with his eyes fixed on the ground looking for frogs, he'd glanced up and seen a glowing light ahead which he thought was the torch of one of his friends. He followed the light deep into the forest but suddenly it went out, leaving him lost, alone and very scared. Granny said my friend had followed *Phi Khamot* a will-o'-the-wisp type of ghost which has no form but glows red at night like a firefly, but with a larger and brighter light. It's a harmless but mischievous ghost and likes to lead travellers astray, leaving them lost and disorientated. If approached, Phi Khamot will immediately disappear.

Phi Phrai is the spirit of a woman who died in childbirth and whose corpse was dug up and used to make a love potion. To make the potion, a sorcerer holds a candle under the corpse's chin and collects the oil that drips from the melting flesh. The oil is then combined with certain herbs and made into a potion which can apparently drive a man wild with lust for the woman who administers it. I've heard that it works just as successfully on a woman, when administered by a man. Understandably, Phi Phrai can get a bit upset about this treatment of her corpse and will try to cause harm to both the sorcerer and the person using the potion, so great precautions have to be taken.

There used to be man-eating tigers in Thailand and they could be the home of an unpleasant ghost called *Suea Saming*. The ghost is that of someone who was eaten by the tiger and now resides in the animal, controlling it. On full moon nights, the ghost makes the tiger take human form, though it can't disguise its tail or lack of fingers. Sometimes it takes the appearance of a beautiful woman and travels to a village or house near the jungle, or it may appear as a relative or friend of someone living in the house. Sometimes the ghost will pretend to be hurt, but it will always find some excuse to lure the householder out of the house and back to the forest, where the ghost changes back into a tiger and eats its victim. A suspicious householder can check whether the late-night caller is real or not by throwing a box of matches out of a window and inviting the caller to light one. The ghost, having no real fingers, cannot hold the match. A similar ghost is *Suea Saming-Akhom*, which as a human was a practitioner of black magic which went wrong and became uncontrollable. The magic returns to the practitioner and causes him to become a man-eating tiger on full moon nights.

Phi Thak Khun is not a specific ghost because *thak khun* describes what many ghosts can do: calling out the name of someone nearby, hoping to gain their attention. It's very unwise to answer or acknowledge the ghost because then it may follow you back home to haunt the house or, if it's a particularly strong ghost, take possession of you. Granny always told me that if I was ever in the forest and heard someone calling my name—even if it sounded like her voice—I must ignore it and run straight home.

One of the most feared and famous ghosts in Thailand is *Phi Tai Tong Klom*: the ghost of a woman who died during childbirth and whose child also died. The ghost is violent and malicious and often kills simply from spite. There is a famous legend of one such Phi Tai Tong Klom. It's a story known to every Thai and has been made and remade for the cinema and television dozens of times, as well as being turned into an opera, a musical and an animated cartoon: the legend of Mae Nak.[8]

Not all Thai ghosts are really 'ghosts' in the normal sense at all, but may simply be the spirit of some natural place, inhabiting large old trees, unusual rock formations, pools of water or the earth itself. If left alone, or given some appropriate offering occasionally, they are often beneficial and return good luck or happiness to the giver. Houses also have their own guardian spirits, which inhabit and protect the gates, stairwells and doorstep (which is why, in Thailand, we always step *over* and not *on* doorsteps). But not all the spirits who live in natural places are friendly or beneficial, as my own childhood experience taught me.

When I was about eight years old, I went with my friend Supot and a few other boys into the forest to forage for food. Our wanderings brought us to a grove, close to a deep, dark pond. None of us had ever been there before. The grove was very silent, damp and gloomy, with many large old trees, vines and rocks. It was quite spooky. We all knew instinctively that it was exactly the sort of place that a forest spirit might inhabit, but none of us were about to admit we were scared, so we continued foraging there. Supot stood on a fallen tree trunk to reach some guava while the rest of us collected fruit from close by. Supot suddenly shouted and fell from the tree trunk on to his back, though his fall was no more than about a metre. We all saw him fall but nobody immediately went to help him because we thought he couldn't possibly be injured, but he seemed to be struggling to get off his back. His arms and legs were waving about but his torso seemed stuck to the ground. After a few minutes he was able to get to his feet but he was angry because he was sure one of us had pinned him down with a foot on his chest. That was obviously impossible because we were nowhere near him.

About a week later we were all playing a ball game in a field when Supot started to complain of severe chest pains and breathing difficulties, as though something was pressing on his chest. He went home but next morning, when I called for him on my way to school, his parents said that he had become very ill during the night and had been taken to the city hospital. His father said Supot was foaming at the mouth and while in a fever called out for each of his friends by name, including me. A day or so later, he died. The doctor thought Supot might have been bitten by a rabid animal but we didn't think so because he would have mentioned it to us and, anyway, he had no bite marks on his body.

Supot's grandfather had a reputation as a Mo Phi and he later questioned all us boys about where we had been recently and what we had done. When we told him about our visit to the spooky glade and described it to him, he immediately knew the place we were talking about. He told us that a very powerful spirit lived in the grove and that Supot's khwan or 'soul' had been taken by the spirit when he fell from the tree. The feeling of someone standing on his chest was the spirit, drawing our friend's khwan from his body. He said that if he had known before Supot died that we had been in that glade, he might have been able to get Supot's khwan back.

At Supot's funeral I ordained as a novice monk for the day to make merit for him. I never went back to that place in the forest again.

Besides spooky glades, deep pools of water or rivers can also be the home of ghosts or spirits. In Granny's childhood, there was a river running close to the village. It was only about six metres wide and quite shallow, so it was possible to wade across, except at one point. At that point the river made a sharp turn in its course and at the turn was a very deep, underwater hole. There were many old stories in the village about how wild elephants used to try and cross the river at that point, and drowned in the hole. There were also many stories about several different spirits or ghosts that lived in the deep water, or nearby.

Granny told me that when she was about ten years old, she and some friends were returning from the paddy fields one late afternoon and saw a woman wearing white sitting on a rock by the river, combing her long white hair. That was odd enough, but what scared Granny and her friends was that as she combed it, the woman's hair became longer and longer and was floating on the surface of the water. The girls ran home, very scared. Next day, when they had to pass that spot again, there was a very large white duck sitting on the same rock, watching them. There were no white ducks in the village, so Granny and her friends were convinced that it was a ghost or spirit of some kind.

Some years later, a villager who lived near that spot was up in a tree collecting coconuts, when he saw a large white shape in the water, close to the big rock. The light was failing and he thought at first it was a huge fish, so he climbed down the tree to take a closer look. When he got there, the object had vanished. He saw the same thing several evenings running. Believing it to be a fish, he decided to wait for it to appear next evening and then shoot it with his musket. The large white shape appeared and the hunter raised his gun and aimed, but even before he put his finger on the trigger, the gun blew up in his face. Some spirits are believed to have the power to control weapons if they are threatened.

In my own childhood, Granny often warned me not to swim in that river and I never did, but when I was about eleven years old, three younger village girls spent an afternoon splashing around in the shallow water near the deep pool. One of the girls was out of the water and standing quite far from the river bank when she suddenly saw a large, dark man-shape walk out of the river and take the arm of her friend, and then lead her back into the water. The girl stayed by the river bank while the third girl ran to get help. When adults arrived and waded into the river, they found the drowned body of the little girl. They later questioned the girl who had seen the ghostly abduction but she just cried and refused to speak. It was only much later that she told her mother that she knew that if she said anything about the dark shape, it would return for her.

The river is still there but it's now little more than a stream and the deep pool has been filled with silt, sand and rock.

Trees, too, have their spirits. All over Thailand, but especially in the far north, there are many huge old trees with brightly coloured cloth wrapped around their trunks, with faded flower garlands and ribbons strung around. Some very old trees may have been wrapped in cloth for decades. At the foot of the tree may be offerings of food, flowers and broken Buddha images. Such trees are the homes of *Phi Ton Mai*; a generic name meaning 'tree ghost'. Illegal felling of old trees is a serious problem in Thailand but nobody would ever knowingly cut down the home of a Phi Ton Mai, so the cloth warns them off. Environmentally conscious Buddhist monks also sometimes wrap a piece of their orange robe around an old tree, in a sense 'ordaining' it, to help protect the tree from illegal cutting. If a tree has to be cut for a valid reason, permission must first be sought from the Phi Ton Mai. To get permission, an axe is left propped against the tree overnight. If the axe is found lying flat on the ground in the morning, the tree cannot be cut. If the axe is still standing in the morning, the Phi Ton Mai has given permission for the tree to be cut, but an alternative home must be found for the spirit.

Not far from my village was one such big old tree, well known to Granny as being the home of a spirit. Not long before I left the village in 1993, the district council started laying the first concrete road nearby. The planned route meant that the tree had to be cut down. A workman arrived with a power-driven chain saw, started it up and approached the tree. The saw cut out. The workman moved away from the tree and powered-up his saw again. As soon as he re-approached the tree it cut out again. The same thing happened several times. The workman, a local man who understood something about spirits, realised what the problem might be and refused to make any more attempts to cut the tree. The road contractor also understood, but he had a job to do and orders to follow, so he called in a bulldozer to knock the tree over by force. As soon as the bulldozer approached the tree, its engine cut out. Eventually, a Ghost Doctor was called in. He performed a simple ritual, made some offerings and explained to the spirit why the tree had to be cut. He then announced to the nervous onlookers that the spirit would allow the tree to be cut only if a spirit house was erected close by, away from the new road, for the spirit to live in. The contractors agreed and the tree was successfully cut down.

Most Phi Ton Mai live in a specific type of tree. *Phi Nang Takhian* is a tree spirit which lives in the Takhian (Hopea) tree. The spirit, known as Lady Takhian, appears as a beautiful woman and sings mournful love songs, hoping to attract a man. When a man investigates the singing, he will find Lady Takhian waiting beneath the tree. She will embrace him so passionately he will suffocate or be squeezed to death. The most dangerous Phi Nang Takhian are those whose trees are close to water and which have roots protruding from the ground. Then, the lady of the tree may be a particularly vicious one. She particularly dislikes men urinating on her roots and I've heard that if she doesn't squeeze you to death, she'll give you ulcers. Granny told me it could have been a Phi Nang Takhian which caused the pain in my friend Supot's chest in the spooky old glade, and from which he later apparently died.

Takhian trees can be very old, so the spirit residing within may also be very old and therefore very powerful. Although the Takhian tree grows to a large size and provides good building timber, Thai people won't use it to construct a house, nor have the tree in their garden, though it is used to make boats.

It's not only old hardwood trees which provide homes for the spirits. According to Granny, *Phi Nang Tani* is a friendly female spirit which lives in banana trees. On a full moon night, she may appear and offer bananas as alms to itinerant monks who pass through the grove, or to men who fall asleep there. But in some old tales Phi Nang Tani seems to have a darker personality and a quite different reputation. In those stories, she appears as a voluptuous and insatiable woman who is said to entice young men into the banana grove at night to feed on their life force, while having wild sex with them. Granny never told me that!

If you hear a strange noise at night
The noise of ghosts, of spirits and demons
Do not call out for it, for it will come for you.
Thai poet Sunthon-Phu (1786-1855)

Have You Eaten Rice Yet?

The first question most Thais will traditionally ask when greeting a friend is: *Where are you going?* The second question will usually be: *Have you eaten rice yet?* The question isn't really about whether the friend has eaten; it's a polite and sincere enquiry about their entire wellbeing, but with a deeper and more complex meaning than the simple: *How are you?*

Millions of Thai people make their living from rice cultivation. Their families may have done so for many hundreds of years. If they traced their ancestry, the vast majority of Thais would find rice farming somewhere in their backgrounds. The grain has been of such importance to Thais for so long that it has become essential for their overall wellbeing, happiness and comfort, to the point where the *concept* of rice has become a significant part of their identity and psyche. For many Thais, rice has great cultural and psychological significance and is an integral part of their personal economy, culture, traditions and religious beliefs, even to the point of being considered almost sacred by the farmers who cultivate it, at least up to my granny's generation. Rice is the staple food of billions of people, but many from industrialised countries who enjoy eating it take the little grains for granted, not realising how much effort, care and even love went into their production.

For some Western city-dwellers, caught up, and perhaps even

trapped, in their busy lives and the hustle, bustle and everyday hassle of modern urban living, the simple farming life might seem idyllic; working outdoors in the fresh air all day, growing your own food, enjoying the fruits of your own labour, sweat of your brow and so on. But it's not like that at all. It's unrelenting and exhausting manual work, often for very little return and, in times of flood, drought or pestilence, sometimes no return at all.

In modern times, with labour-saving mechanical devices like tractors, quick-growing strains of rice and chemical fertilisers and pesticides to improve crop yield, much has improved since Granny's day and since my own childhood in the village. But even now, for impoverished farmers who can't afford to retire their buffaloes and invest in a tractor, with the associated and rising cost of fuel and maintenance, nor the cost of modern fertilisers, automatic water pumps or other mechanical aids, rice farming still remains back-breaking manual work, just as it has always been. Those farmers who are persuaded to borrow money from banks to mechanise (so reducing their labour, increasing their yield and theoretically raising their standard of living) often find themselves poorer than they were before: trapped in an endless cycle of poverty, debt and more poverty. In very recent years, some farmers in my village have lost their land to banks or money-lenders—land which may have been in their families for centuries.

Granny's generation was almost the last of the traditional rice farmers. Until then, farming skills had been handed down from generation to generation without significant change. The tools of the trade had always been buffalo-drawn wooden ploughs, hoes, sickles and manual threshing—plus a strong back, nimble hands and prayers and rituals for rain and a good harvest. In Granny's day, rice farming had a very strong spiritual element. Toiling with one's own hands and in such close proximity and harmony with the earth and the rice created a personal and spiritual relationship to the crop and to the environment. The spirits of the fields and the rice were traditionally respected and placated at every stage of cultivation. For modern farmers, with their mechanised and more impersonal methods, the ancient traditions must seem rather old-fashioned and unnecessary. Many have been forgotten, except in the most remote areas.

When Granny first started working in the paddy fields in 1930, when she was nine years old, one rice crop a year was normal throughout Thailand. Now, with new rice strains, combine harvesters and better irrigation and drainage systems, two and even three crops a year are possible in some regions. In my own village in Uttaradit in the lower north, only one crop of rice is still harvested. Only a minority of farmers in the village can afford to mechanise but in recent times some have diversified and now grow a wider variety of cash crops, including sweet corn, onions and green beans.

The rice growing season has regional variations depending on soil quality, rainfall and local tradition. In my home province the growing season begins in May and ends in July, while harvesting begins in November and ends in December. Farming methods also vary slightly from region to region, but they all follow the same basic procedures. There are many stages involved and each is essential for a successful harvest. In Granny's day, traditional rituals and offerings at each stage were just as essential and most were aimed at pleasing or placating one particular spirit: *Mae Phosop*—the Rice Mother. Mae Phosop lives in the rice plant and in every grain. She is rather sensitive and easily offended, especially if her grains are abused or mistreated by humans. Then, according to Granny, she can get quite sulky and the rice crop might fail.

On my ninth birthday, Granny took me with her early in the morning to the paddy fields. Thai people measure the stages of life in twelve-year cycles but the number nine is also considered lucky and significant. I was born on the ninth day of the month, so maybe Granny thought my ninth birthday was a good time to share some of her folk-wisdom with me; a sort of coming-of-age chat. I'm glad about that now because she never lived to see my first cycle, or twelfth birthday.

Granny and I sat down side by side in the early morning sun, looking out over the fields, with me a little puzzled as to why we were there. We sat in silence for a while and then she laid her wrinkled old hand over mine and said she had something important to explain to me. She was very serious, as though she was about to impart some ancient and arcane knowledge, which to her way of thinking she was. She said I had to understand why rice was so essential in our lives, not simply as our staple food but as the very foundation of our existence, just as it had been in our family for hundreds of years. She then told me the story of Mae Phosop; the spirit and mother of the rice which bound us together as a family, a community and a nation. Granny said that whether I believed her story or not, if I wanted to be a successful farmer I had to understand that every grain of rice was important and had to be respected and cared for at each stage of its growth, as though it was our own child.

There are many ancient legends about Mae Phosop. The one Granny passed on to me was that Mae Phosop was originally an angel and the consort of a god. She enjoyed gardening and growing things in her heavenly realm but one day, seeing that she was becoming old, her god-husband suggested that she should donate her flesh as rice to mankind. She did so and fell to earth as rice seed. She became the Rice Mother.

According to the legend, in ancient times rice grains were as big as a man's forearm and had the magical power to fly into the rice stores by themselves. At the end of one rice growing season, a farmer hadn't prepared her rice store in time for the arrival of the grains and was busy getting it ready. The rice grains flew in unexpectedly, surprising the woman so much that she lashed out at them with a wooden pole. Mae Phosop was so frightened and annoyed at the treatment of her grains that she left the earth and retired sulking to her heavenly realm. Because she had abandoned the paddy fields, the rice crop failed the following year and famine followed. Mae Phosop only returned to Earth after farmers starting making offerings and performing rituals to keep her happy. Granny told me that these offerings should be made at every stage of the cultivation of the rice but are most important when Mae Phosop might think the rice seedlings or grains are being abused, especially when farmers harvest with sharp sickles, or when threshing.

In other parts of the country, the Mae Phosop legend has been linked to the Buddha. According to that story, Mae Phosop was once more respected and more popular than the Buddha. She felt the respect was justified, since as the Rice Mother she had been born before any of the Buddhas had appeared on Earth and her rice grains had provided food for all of them. But as more and more people came to hear the new Buddha's teachings, they paid less attention and less respect to Mae Phosop. She was offended and hid herself away. The Buddha later sent messengers to find her. They persuaded Mae Phosop to return by promising that in future all people would pay respect to her by offering a wai (the Thai hand gesture of respect) after eating rice. Mae Phosop agreed and returned. Many older Thais still wai Mae Phosop at the end of every meal.

Partly because of these ancient legends, most traditional Thai farmers still do respect the rice very much and would never abuse or misuse even a single grain. Granny taught me that I must never offend Mae Phosop by spitting or urinating in the rice fields, by wasting rice, by dropping it on the floor or by stepping on it or over it and that I should accord it—and therefore Mae Phosop— the same respect that I would show to my own mother. Granny said that even when I had to feed the family chickens, the rice should always be placed in a container and not just scattered on the ground. Sadly, that level of respect for the rice has largely been forgotten by younger Thais. In modern times, rice has become just another packaged commodity bought at the supermarket.

Even with regular offerings to Mae Phosop, the rice still can't grow without sufficient water. It's obviously very important for farmers that rain should fall on time and when most needed. In my province it usually did. When I lived in the village there was never a year when there was a drought or even insufficient rain, but Granny could remember some years in her own youth when the rain was late or there wasn't enough of it. Then, the rice crop failed and all the villagers suffered great hardship.

Just before the theoretical start of each rainy season, Granny would be constantly watching and reading the sky. One year, when it looked as though the rains might be late, she told me to find a large female cat and to keep it nearby in case she needed it. I asked her what she wanted it for. She wouldn't tell me but the cat wasn't needed anyway because the rain arrived soon after. She probably didn't want to tell me because, as I discovered many years later, the ritual she had in mind with the cat had a vaguely sexual connotation.

The ritual is called *Hae Nang Maeow*. I don't think it's held much anymore but in Granny's day it was common throughout Thailand, especially in the northeast and amongst people of Lao descent. The ritual was performed at the beginning of the rainy season if the expected rain wasn't on time or was insufficient to get the crops growing. It could be held at different times in different parts of Thailand, depending on rainfall in that particular area, and might be held several times before the desired affect was achieved. I never saw the ritual performed in my own village but later, in my university days, I observed it when I had to research local folklore in Nakhon Sawan Province, in the lower northern region. My research was in a tiny Lao village in a very remote area and I arrived just after the theoretical start of the rainy season. There hadn't been much rain so far and the villagers were worried that they might be facing drought. Time to get the cat out!

A female cat (symbolising fertility) was placed in an escape-prove bamboo basket shaped something like a throne. The basket was suspended between two wooden poles, like an emperor's palanquin, and carried on the shoulders of four men. The cat in the ritual I saw was black, though a grey one is apparently better because it has the same colour as rain clouds. Grey cats are quite rare in Thailand and sometimes you have to make do.

The strange ritual started late in the afternoon at the village monastery, where the monks were chanting to make rain. When the chanting was finished, the caged cat was carried through the village, accompanied by a procession of loudly wailing villagers and a band banging drums and cymbals, making as much noise as possible. It was not only a very loud parade but also a bit wobbly, since the men carrying the palanquin had drunk a considerable amount of rice whisky and could hardly stand upright. Along the route, the villagers (mostly elderly ladies very much like Granny) danced frenziedly around the palanquin wailing at the tops of their voices and shaking large, round bamboo trays, usually used for sifting rice. But the point of the parade was to get the cat itself to make a lot of noise to attract the attention of the male rain gods, reminding them to send rain to impregnate the female gods of the earth. The best way to make a cat howl is to throw water over it, so at every house villagers came out with bowls, jugs or buckets and drenched the poor cat. Everybody—except the cat—thought this was great fun. The parade ended back at the monastery where the cat, soaked but unharmed, was set free. Oddly enough, the day after the parade there was a cloud burst and the village was flooded.

Provided that the rains were expected to be on time, the cycle of rice cultivation always began by preparing the new season's seed grains. In every family rice store in the village there were always a few sacks of the best rice grains saved for the next season's planting. In my family's stores the special grain was kept in thick hessian sacks, tightly tied. Just before the first rains were due we would take the sacks to the local canal and immerse them in the water. Within days, the rice had started to show its first tiny roots and shoots.

While the seeds were soaking, the fields had to be ploughed and prepared for planting, starting with one which was to be used as a nursery field. My family's nursery field covered about twenty percent of the total area to be planted. Ploughing was done immediately after the first light showers of the rainy season, when the iron-hard earth had been softened a little. I usually helped my father with the ploughing and it was exhausting work, taking four or five days, even though the heavy wooden plough was drawn by a buffalo. My family didn't own a buffalo of their own but in those days wealthier village neighbours were very generous about lending their work beasts, sometimes in return for manual work on their own land. Neighbours were always willing to help each other out so ploughing and other major work was usually staggered by each family, to give us all time to get the work done together.

Ploughing was the symbolic opening of the rice-growing season, so then Granny made the first of her offerings to Mae Phosop. She and my mother would go to the fields early in the morning, wearing their best clothes and carrying plates of betel, areca nut, tobacco, food, incense and flowers. They would kneel in the centre of the newly ploughed, muddy paddies and quietly entreat Mae Phosop to send a good harvest. The offerings were then laid under a big old tree at the edge of the field. In nearby fields, other ladies could be seen doing exactly the same thing. Looking back, I realise how touching and sincere the scene was and how perfectly it illustrated the old-time farmers' relationship to the land and the crop.

The opening of the rice growing season is very significant in Thailand, since the livelihood of millions of farmers depends on a good crop. His Majesty The King even presides over an important and ancient ploughing ceremony to mark the day.[9]

After ploughing, we then had to make the fields flat with a hoe. That also took several days and it was important to get it right. The earth had to be as flat as possible to ensure even water distribution, but with a very slight slope to help drainage.

The irrigation and drainage canals for the fields also had to be repaired and re-dug before planting could begin, since too little or too much water can destroy the rice. A large field was partitioned into smaller plots, with raised earth walls around each. The walls trapped water within the plots but could be quickly broken down to drain them, in the event of excessive rainfall. The water level in the flooded paddies could not be allowed to reach higher than the lowest leaves on the young plants, which was about two or three centimetres.

When the fields were ready, we would haul the heavy wet sacks of grain out of the canal and the seedlings would be scattered into the flooded nursery field, but without making any attempt to get the grain in neat furrows. After a month or so, the rice seedlings would have grown to about thirty centimetres. Granny and my mother would then pull them up and arrange them into very neat small bunches. About a third of the top of each bunch was cut off to allow new leaves to grow. The young plants were then ready for transplanting into the other fields. At that time Granny made more offerings to Mae Phosop, to let her know what was happening to her young plants.

Although ploughing was usually done by the men, transplanting into the flooded fields was traditionally women's work, probably because of their female connection to Mae Phosop. It was hot, sweaty, back-breaking labour involving days of being constantly bent double, which is why so many elderly rural ladies, like Granny, had permanently damaged spines and walking difficulties in their later years. I usually helped Granny and my mother with transplanting but it wasn't as easy as it looked. Each bunch of seedlings is held between the thumb and the first and second fingers of one hand, with the tips of the fingers forming a point. The joined fingers are then plunged into the thick mud, making a small hole into which the plants are gently pushed. This process had to be repeated many thousands of times before the fields were completely planted. The seedlings were placed an exact distance apart (usually about twenty centimetres in my village) but the skill came not only in planting at the correct distance but also in ensuring that the fragile roots were perfectly straight in the mud. If they weren't, the young plant could die. In her more than fifty years of working in the fields, Granny probably planted *millions* of rice seedlings.

Working in the muddy water all day brought other problems besides backache. The women worked barefooted, so when Granny and my mother left the fields at the end of the day they would usually have to scrape leeches from their feet and legs. Water snakes were also a constant danger because they all bite and some are venomous. In modern times the women sensibly wear rubber boots. Transplanting was a task that the village women joyfully shared. Because it was such a lot of work, they all helped out in each other's fields, which gave a great sense of cooperation, harmony and community.

After transplanting, it was then mainly a matter of waiting for the plants to grow but while they were becoming established we had to keep a constant watch on the water level in the paddies. If bad weather was likely, one of the family would stay overnight in the fields in a temporary open-sided bamboo shack, so we could react quickly in case of sudden flooding, which could drown and kill the young plants. If that happened, the paddy field had to be immediately drained to the correct level, even if it meant working at night in the pouring rain. Too little rain brought its own problems: the available water had to be constantly recirculated from one field to another, to wherever it was most urgently needed. In Granny's day all irrigation was done by manually breaking down the dirt walls of the paddy fields and by cutting ditches. Although our traditional methods seem very primitive now that most farmers uses automatic pumps, Granny had many years of experience in water management and she knew exactly where to cut a ditch, place a dam, or make a hole in the field wall.

Over the next three or four months the rice plants were left to grow in the flooded paddy fields and slowly turned from emerald green to a darker green, and then to golden brown. They needed constant nurturing during that time. We had to be especially vigilant to make sure that insects didn't attack the young plants and each one was carefully inspected every day. In modern times chemical insecticides are used, but Granny made her own nontoxic pesticide using the very bitter leaves from the Nim tree, which is a member of the mahogany family. The leaves were boiled with other natural ingredients before being added to the water in the field. I used to help Granny mix the herbal brew and I distinctly remember its horrible smell, but it worked very well. Nim didn't actually kill the insects, it simply drove them away. We never had to use chemical fertiliser on the fields because the buffaloes provided huge quantities of natural fertiliser. The soil in my province was excellent then and always produced a good crop, though most local farmers do now use chemical fertilisers, partly at least because their own chemical pesticides have adversely affected the soil.

When the plants started to produce their little grains, Mae Phosop was assumed to be pregnant. Granny, being the village midwife, knew that mothers-to-be need to be pampered, so at that time she would offer a variety of special gifts and food that the

Rice Mother was believed to particularly enjoy and which helped prevent morning sickness.

To prepare the offering, Granny had to make a special bamboo basket called a *chalom*, shaped rather like a tall onion. The top of the finished basket was decorated with flowers, incense and a small triangular paper flag. The basket was then lined with banana leaves before being filled with the gifts. Nobody in my village now remembers why the gifts had to be offered in this way and I don't think even Granny knew, but she followed the tradition, just as her own mother and grandmother had done. The gifts included a mirror, a comb, scented water, specially prepared curries, sticky rice and sweets. To make the offering, Granny drove a bamboo pole into the earth (the pole had to be taller than the level of the rice) and tied the basket to it with a length of bamboo twine. She then poured the scented water over the rice plants while talking very gently to them, asking Mae Phosop to produce many healthy grains.

There was one other gift in Granny's basket that she said Mae Phosop particularly enjoyed when she was pregnant: an orange. Oranges were not grown in my region but could occasionally be bought from fruit sellers who passed through the village. Oranges were very expensive but Granny obviously thought the expense was worthwhile. So did I. Food offered to the spirits cannot be taken back but after a couple of days I would sneak into the field and run off with the prized orange, eating it secretly in the forest. The rice crop never failed so I assume Mae Phosop, being a mother, understood that little boys can be greedy.

During the growing period the muddy fields attracted a variety of creatures, many of them helpfully feeding on insects or on each other. Rats, fish, crabs, giant water beetles, eels and snakes were very common and they were all a good free food source for the family. They were very easy to catch in Granny's ingenious and varied bamboo traps, but my young friends and I liked to turn foraging into a game. We children were absolutely forbidden by our parents to play in the fields in case we damaged the fragile rice plants but of course, with so much free food running, crawling or slithering around, we couldn't resist. We would sneak commando-style on our bellies into a neighbour's fields (never into our own) and wriggle our way in the thick mud through the rows of plants, with small covered bamboo baskets on our backs. We had to be very careful to keep a low profile because the farmers kept a constant lookout on the fields from their shelters. By digging our hands into the mud, we could usually pull out a crab or an eel and then quickly transfer it to our basket. Fish were just as easy to catch because they couldn't escape fast enough through the thick rice plants. Our game had its dangers, though. I once pulled out from the mud what I thought at first glance was a large eel, until its forked tongue flickered at me. I was holding a venomous water snake.

By mid-November, when the rice was nearly fully grown, it was time to decide when to harvest it. Granny had an almost uncanny knowledge and understanding of rice. She would look carefully at the grains and was able to predict exactly when they would be perfectly ripe. She would never say something vague like *sometime next week*, but always gave the precise number of days and then insist that it had to be done on that particular day; not a day before nor a day after. She was always right and our rice grains were always perfect.

Before the rice could be harvested, Granny had to make yet another Mae Phosop offering, this time because the rice plants were about to be cut with sharp sickles—Mae Phosop is apparently very frightened of knives. While she was making the offerings, Granny would talk to the rice plants and explain to the Rice Mother what was about to happen, to keep the sensitive spirit calm. The plants were then cut and left on the ground for a day or two to dry, before being bundled into neat sheaves prior to threshing. At that time, Granny would entreat Mae Phosop to leave the paddy fields and join the cut stalks in the threshing area.

These days there are always concrete areas in villages which make ideal threshing grounds. In my childhood, we didn't have a suitable place in the village itself so each family had to prepare one of their fields for the task. For my family's threshing, we first flattened and leveled an area about ten metres square with hoes. I then had the job of spreading liquefied buffalo dung over the area. That had to be done several times, with each layer being left to dry, until I finally had a hard, glazed surface. The coating of dried dung prevented grains from falling into the earth or dirt from getting mixed with the grains. It was an unpleasant job but I didn't mind because I was always paid for my work; one-baht per day was the going rate.

Once the surface was dry and hard, we surrounded the threshing ground with crude scarecrows. They were just bamboo poles with a cross-bar and a few of my old clothes draped over them, but they were very effective in keeping birds away from the grain. In some regions, instead of scarecrows, a tall bamboo pole is raised in the centre of the threshing area, with an umbrella of thorny branches fixed to it. With the area prepared, the sheaves of rice were stacked up in a circle around it, but of course threshing couldn't begin until Granny had made another Mae Phosop offering.

Like the harvesting with sickles, the threshing process had to be explained to Mae Phosop because of her sensitivity to the way humans treated her grains. The rice stalks were about to be trampled on and beaten, so she had to be placated. Granny made a little doll-like representation of Mae Phosop from straw and put it in the centre of the threshing ground, so the Rice Mother could watch what was going on.

With Mae Phosop in a relaxed mood, our threshing could begin. Individual stalks were taken from the sheaves and laid in layers in a circle around the threshing ground. Borrowed buffaloes were then walked in a circle around the area, treading on the stalks, so their heavy weight separated out the grains of rice. I also joined in by trampling on the stalks. This method of threshing, by walking buffaloes over the rice stalks, is still used by some farmers in my village, though the wealthier ones now drive their tractors over the stalks.

When the first stalks were considered well-threshed, it was my job to remove them from the threshing ground and lay down new ones. Later, the already buffalo-threshed stalks would be further beaten with sticks, to remove any grains still clinging on. Every single grain was important and had to be collected, so I had to scour the threshing area and surrounding field in case even one had escaped. Granny would follow along after me, to make sure I hadn't missed any. Her eyes were not so good as she got older but Granny could still spot a single rice grain from several metres away. Finally, any dirt, non-grain materials or immature grains were removed from the rice, which was spread out and left to dry before being taken to the family rice store. (It's not unusual these days to drive down a country road and find half the concrete surface covered with someone's rice crop, drying in the sun.)

Remembering what had happened in ancient times, when Mae Phosop was offended by a farmer who didn't properly prepare the rice store, Granny would invite the Rice Mother to inspect the store before the rice was placed in it. She would make another small straw image of Mae Phosop and leave it in the store with offerings which this time included a boiled egg, water and sweets, and then invite Mae Phosop to take a look. If Mae Phosop didn't make her unhappiness known, the rice was poured in. The grain skin was left on, because that helped protect the rice from fungus. When we wanted to use the rice, the skin would be removed by pounding or grinding the grains in a bamboo milling machine, handmade by Granny, and then sieved in a large, circular bamboo tray.

And so ended another successful and plentiful rice harvest, with sufficient rice stored to keep the family fed for another year.

During my occasional return visits to the village, I am always surprised at the changes that have come about since I left in 1993. The stages in cultivating the rice are exactly the same but the methods and tools have changed dramatically. Many of the buffaloes used for ploughing have been retired and the old wooden ploughs and buffalo carts have been broken up, sold to city antique dealers or sent to museums. Tractors and even one or two combine harvesters now buzz busily and efficiently around the fields. There are very few ladies of my granny's generation left and they are now very old indeed. One ninety-year-old lady told me that she still performs the Mae Phosop rites and makes offerings to the spirit, just as her own granny did, but she will probably be one of the last ever to do so. Her grandchildren, and all the grandchildren of the village, with their hi-tech farming methods, have taken control of the fields and of nature itself and don't need the Rice Mother's help. Or perhaps they do, but simply don't realise it.

Once the rice harvest was over, there was less work to do in the fields but always plenty of other jobs to keep farmers occupied. As soon as they could be spared, many of the men would then take temporary labouring jobs in the cities, to earn extra cash. During that quiet time, I would often go fishing in a nearby canal after getting home from school.

One evening when I told Granny I was going fishing, she decided she would join me. Women traditionally didn't forage or hunt for food, which was considered men's work, but fishing was acceptable. My homemade fishing rod was just a short, thin bamboo pole, some cotton line, a wooden float and a hook baited with a worm. Granny and I sat side by side on the edge of the canal and I cast my line. Nothing happened for about half an hour. I told Granny the fish weren't biting and that we might as well go home. She asked me if she could have a try. She took the line off the rod, fixed the hook onto the end of the rod and threw away the bait. She'd brought some rice dust with her from home and she scattered it on the surface of the water. She tapped the rod lightly onto the surface and then immediately gave it a sharp flick. A fish flew out of the water and over her shoulder. A few seconds later, another one. Then another. She pulled out about a dozen fish in less than a minute. I was running around trying to collect all these flapping fish from the grassy bank, and they just kept coming; *flick, flick, flick*. It was amazing. I asked Granny if I could try her method. She smiled and passed me the rod. I couldn't catch a thing. I'm not suggesting there was anything magical about Granny's fishing method, but it was some strange skill that I was never able to learn.

Besides fishing, one of my favourite evening pastimes was to ride a buffalo. Buffaloes were very important in our small community then and essential to our way of life and to our survival. I saw them every day and they were just part of my village environment. I suppose I took them for granted and to me, as a child, they were friendly but rather dull and stupid animals. Granny once tried to tell me otherwise, but it was to be many years after she died that I understood what she meant.

Swamp buffaloes, or water buffaloes as they are usually known, are wonderful animals. Because of their huge, broad feet, buffaloes are the only creatures fully adapted to working in the muddy paddies, but they don't have to be enticed to work, or forced with ill-treatment. Although most Thai farmers view their buffaloes simply as working animals, rather than sentimentally as pets, they *never* mistreat them and do seem to have a genuine respect for them. Once trained, buffaloes simply plod along, hour after hour, year after year, always reliable and never showing tiredness or bad temper. In my experience, they never bite, kick or become excited, unless startled. They are also massive, especially to a little boy, but because they are so gentle I was never frightened of them, even when I was a toddler.

At the end of a long day working in the paddy fields, buffaloes had to be fed on fresh grass and given a good wash in the canal. Farmers were usually too exhausted to do this important duty themselves but the village boys were more than happy to help out. Riding a big buffalo through the fields and washing it in the canal are amongst my happiest childhood memories.

My young friends and I would often rush home from school to take neighbours' buffaloes for their evening feed and wash, each of us hoping to get the biggest animal. A big, old buffalo can weigh up to about 600 kilos, though wild buffaloes, of which there are still a few in Thailand, can be even heavier. They're easy to ride, though their great protruding bellies mean that a child must usually lay flat on the animal's back to ride it, or sit on its shoulders. On many evenings, a group of four or five of us boys would ride the huge creatures to good grassy or weedy areas. As the buffaloes plodded along, the large, antique wooden bells hung around their broad necks would make delightful hollow *klonk klonk* sounds, each with a slightly different tone depending on the size of the bell, but the individual tones making each buffalo easy to identify. While the buffaloes were eating, we could leave them and go foraging nearby for food ourselves, because the oldest and biggest buffalo would automatically keep control of the younger ones. Afterwards, when the buffaloes had eaten enough, we would ride on to the canal to wash them, while climbing or laying on their broad backs. Buffaloes love being immersed in water and they seem to have a naturally good relationship with children, so I think they enjoyed these excursions as much as we did.

I'm not sure if this has any scientific basis, but Granny told me that buffaloes can remember individual humans by their smell. That was also my own experience. I rode the same old buffalo many times and it would always nuzzle and sniff me in a very friendly way for a moment before I climbed on its back, whereas a new buffalo would likely be more nervous and skittish with me. I also think that buffaloes dislike certain colours or shades, even though I've read that they are colour blind. Several times, on return visits to the village as a novice monk, wearing my orange robes, I was chased by buffaloes which didn't seem to like the colour at all. One time I even had to take refuge in a tree, until the buffaloes got bored and wandered away.

Buffaloes live to about twenty-five years old and have a working life of about fourteen years. In modern times, older buffaloes are usually slaughtered for meat, but that rarely happened in Granny's day. Then, the animal was retired from work and when it eventually died it was buried with great respect, though without particular ceremony. Usually the farmer would dig a very deep hole in the forest, or on some unused land, carefully bury the carcass and leave an offering of incense, grass and water for the spirit of the animal.

According to government figures, there were about seven million buffaloes in Thailand in 1980, the year I was born. By 2007, the number had shrunk to under two million. The total rice production area in Thailand also shrunk during that time as more and more farmers sold their paddy fields to developers for use as industrial estates or housing estates, or turned their land over to cattle breeding. Many small farm holders also changed to growing other crops besides rice, for which buffaloes were not always needed. Although there were several reasons for the declining buffalo numbers, the increased use of tractors was a major factor.

Granny and I saw a tractor for the first time in about 1985, when I was five years old. A wealthy farmer in a nearby village had bought one and my family and many neighbours went to take a look at this marvellous machine. All of us, including Granny, were impressed at how quickly, efficiently and effortlessly it could plough a field, compared to a plodding buffalo pulling a wooden plough. The farmer was delighted with his new purchase and was the envy of the community. A couple of years later, Granny told me that she saw the same farmer ploughing his fields with a borrowed buffalo. His tractor had broken down and he didn't have the money to get it fixed. Knowing Granny, I think she was probably secretly pleased about that. Although she didn't doubt the efficiency of tractors, I think she probably had misgivings about their lack of *spiritual connection* to the earth and to the rice. That was very important to her.

Once, when I innocently suggested that my family should borrow money to buy a tractor, Granny snorted derisively and asked: *And what does a tractor return to the Earth Mother?* The answer, of course, is nothing, whereas buffaloes constantly fertilise the land with huge quantities of dung, which is free of toxic chemical residues. Unlike tractors, buffaloes rarely break down and cost nothing to maintain or feed and they produce more free buffaloes. It just doesn't seem to make sense for small farm holders to even consider buying a tractor. I think if Granny had had the money and the choice between buying a tractor or a buffalo, she would certainly have chosen the buffalo, despite the extra work that would entail.

All is not lost for Thailand's buffaloes or traditional rice farming methods. With the spiralling cost of fuel and chemical fertilisers, some small farm holders are now actually selling their tractors and going back to ploughing in the traditional way. Even the Thai Ministry of Agriculture is considering ways to increase the use of buffaloes and natural fertiliser. I think Granny would be very happy about that.

I think she would also be happy that many years after she tried to give me a particular lesson, I finally got the message. Granny had a very realistic view about the farming life. To her, and to all farmers, buffaloes were working animals. They weren't mistreated but they were worked very hard indeed, until they were too old to work anymore. That was exactly the same fate for the farmers themselves.

When I was about ten years old, I returned home one day after feeding and watering a buffalo and told Granny what a good time we both had. Granny said something which at the time seemed very strange to me; very *Granny*. She told me that next time I took a buffalo out, I should look deep into the creature's eyes. Next day, I did so. She asked me in the evening what I had seen. I replied something like: *Just a stupid old buffalo*. Granny said nothing, but shook her head resignedly. I was reminded of that many years later, when I lived in a city.

I was sitting at a roadside food stall one evening when a mahout came by, selling bananas and sugarcane to be fed to a young elephant which followed morosely behind him. Elephants should never be brought into the city, with the dangers of traffic, but now that they're rarely employed in the logging industry, mahouts and their elephants have to try to make an alternative living. I was stroking the elephant's head and happened to look deep into its eyes. I saw the same thing there that I had seen in the old buffalo's eyes. This is going to sound a bit fanciful but I felt as though I was looking into the elephant's soul—and seeing nothing but despair. I was actually quite upset. I understood then what Granny wanted me to know about our good friend the buffalo. Like the elephant it is a very noble creature, it is not dull or stupid and it has feelings. It understands its lot in life and is willing to work hard, but it must *always* be treated with great kindness, respect and, perhaps, even love.

There was much I enjoyed about the farming life and working with my family in the fields. It was very hard work but it seemed a simple, harmless and traditional way to make a living, albeit a basic one. Before I started to become more interested in studying, my family thought that farming would be my life. So did I. But I knew from a very young age that farming and living in a village community wasn't just about growing things. Sometimes animals had to be killed, though I'd been taught by Granny never to be cruel to any living creature. However, one day when I was about ten years old, Granny decided that I should have a lesson in a more brutal side of farming. Granny heard that a neighbour was going to have a young calf castrated. That makes the animal docile, more controllable and more suitable as a working beast, since it grows larger and stronger. Granny decided that I was old enough to watch. In retrospect it was unpleasant, though I didn't think so at the time.

Castration was done by a specialist, always a man. Not every community had such a specialist, but one could usually be called in from some nearby village. The fee was usually fixed at less than one baht—twenty-five or fifty satang—but the specialists preferred to be paid in a combination of the low value coins because of their gold colour. Traditionally castration was only done on Mondays, Wednesdays and Fridays and never on Buddhist Holy Days.

Like most activities in the community, the castration couldn't go ahead until a ritual had been performed and offerings made. They included a candle, incense sticks, tobacco and a dried coconut. The castrator also prepared a mixture of coconut oil and herbs, which were to be used to help heal the calf's wound afterwards. The oil and herbs were slowly cooked together, while the castrator prayed to the spirits, asking forgiveness for what he was about to do. He then chanted a spell over the calf to relax the animal. In the castration I saw, the calf became immediately and strangely calm after the chanting. The animal had to be held tightly to prevent it struggling after the castration, so it was bound between two heavy wooden stakes, one on each side of its shoulders and with its feet roped to nearby trees. Two thin bamboo sticks were placed either side of its testicles, which were pulled out from between its rear legs. The sticks were then twisted at the base of the testicles to make them more prominent. Three or four quick blows from a wooden coconut hammer were used to crush the testicles, accompanied by much wincing from the young men watching. The coconut oil and herbs were immediately smeared over the wound, which healed very quickly. Some other specialists might remove the testicles entirely, but that wasn't common in my village.

I know it sounds barbaric these days, but exactly the same method of animal castration was used in rural communities in the West until fairly recent times. Happily, the method isn't used anymore in my village, since there are now more scientific, humane and painless ways of achieving the aim.

It was just part of village life.

Silly Superstition
or Something More?

Superstitions, myths, legends, old wives' tales—where and how do they begin? My Granny *was* an old wife and she once told me an apparently true tale about something that has since become a legend in my village; a shadow of a forgotten truth. It was the story of the 'little people' of the forest. If this story is true—and I have no reason to doubt it—it could be of some anthropological significance.

When I was about eight years old, Granny and I were walking through a fairly dense part of a forest one afternoon. The forest was dark and gloomy at any time of the day and Granny needed my young eyes to spot a particular plant she wanted for one of her herbal medicines. We were following the trail of a wild pig or deer, our eyes fixed on the ground, when Granny suddenly stopped dead. She whispered to me not to move and to make no sound. She slowly raised her eyes and stared fixedly ahead into a dark and almost impenetrable clump of trees. I was terrified, thinking there might be a tiger in there, but after about a minute or so Granny relaxed and shook her head resignedly. 'What was it?' I asked, 'What did you see?' Granny replied that she wasn't sure what it was, but she was *hoping* it might have been a pygmy of a very particular tribe that hadn't been seen around the village for more than fifty years: *Maeng-an-lom*. In our local Khammueang language, Maeng-an-lom meant 'small-bent-falling'. The fact that such a descriptive name was given to the pygmies seems to at least partly bear out the strange tale that Granny then told me.

The Maeng-an-lom seem to have been unique to our lower northern region and perhaps lived only in our province, or even only in the dense forests surrounding our community. What made them unique, and which led to their strange name, was their feet. This sounds impossible, but Granny told me their feet went almost straight from sole to ankle and seemed to have no obvious heel at all, so the pygmies walked bent forward, balanced on their toes. Without a heel, if they tried to stand upright, they would fall over backwards—hence *bent and falling*. Despite that, Granny said, they were able to run very fast on their tip-toes if frightened.

Granny told me that in about 1926, when she was five years old, she was very startled to see two very old male pygmies walk into the village, bent forward, bare-footed and walking on their toes. They were thin and wiry, about 120 centimetres tall, dark-skinned and clothed only in belts and loincloths made of leaves and bark. (She never said whether they carried any sort of spear, bow or other weapons.) Granny ran frightened to her grandmother, who told her that the pygmies were harmless and had only come to beg for rice. She said they lived in the deep forest and rarely came to the village anymore, though when Granny's granny was a child (which would have been around 1860–1870) they were more frequently seen. In her young days, a group of six or eight old men would occasionally turn up, sometimes with a wild pig to trade for rice. They spoke an almost unintelligible language and were neither friendly nor aggressive, but were very shy. Because of the small amount of rice the men wanted, Granny's granny guessed that there were probably only a few dozen of them in all, living in the forest. She said that over the years they were seen less often and in decreasing numbers. The visit to the village by the two men in about 1926, when my granny was a child, was the last time they were ever seen.

According to Granny's granny, the Maeng-an-lom lived in an almost impenetrable forest only a few kilometres from the village, but they moved camp frequently and were rarely observed in their natural habitat. It was known that they didn't live in settlements or build permanent dwellings but instead made temporary shelters from large leaves. As soon as the leaves started to turn yellow, they moved on a short distance and made new shelters. This part of the story is reminiscent of another Thai ethnic group, the *Mlabri*, though they are not pygmies.[10] The Maeng-an-lom didn't farm or cultivate their own food but were excellent hunters, being able to move on their toes totally silently through the forest. Granny's granny said that they also had the ability to immediately recognise any part of the forest they had previously travelled through, in which case they could move very quickly. If it was a new and unknown part of the forest, they moved more slowly and carefully. Although the Maeng-an-lom were rarely seen, hunters from the village occasionally reported a feeling of being watched while they were in the forest, but the pygmies had the ability to fade into the background and become almost invisible.

Granny had never forgotten her own brief childhood encounter with the two pygmies and longed all her life to meet the Maeng-an-lom again, to try to talk with them and learn about them. She told me, very sadly, that she thought they had probably all died.

Although pygmies, or negritos, are known in Thailand, I

can find no reference to any tribe living in the lower northern or central region, nor to any tribe anywhere in the world which has such strangely formed feet. Yet Granny claimed to have seen the Maeng-an-lom and their feet for herself, just as her own granny had. If the story is true, it seems possible that the Maeng-an-lom were an entirely undiscovered tribe, known only to the residents of my village.

The story of the Maeng-an-lom is well known to all the older people in the village, having been passed on to them by their mothers and grandmothers, and is accepted as fact. Amongst the younger folk, the story has started to become a myth—an old wives' tale—and will likely soon be forgotten entirely.

This strange tale has an even more bizarre twist, with an event that would have happened (if it happened at all) probably somewhere between 1890–1900. According to Granny's granny, the Maeng-an-lom gradually became less welcome in the village after chickens started to disappear at night. It didn't happen often and the chickens could have been taken by snakes, but the pygmies were suspected. When some of his own chickens disappeared, Granny's grandfather decided to confront the Maeng-an-lom, though he knew he had little chance of finding them in the forest. He went anyway, carrying his musket as usual, though he intended no harm against the pygmies. Deep in the forest, instead of meeting the Maeng-an-lom, he claimed he suddenly came face to face with a giant humanoid, standing upright and eating bamboo shoots. The thick forest would probably have been very gloomy but according to Granny's grandfather, the creature was between two and three metres tall and seemed very dark, as though possibly covered in hair. Very frightened, he took a shot at it, but thought he missed. He ran for his life, but the creature seemed more frightened than him and ran off in the opposite direction.

These days, the legend of Bigfoot is known worldwide and doubtless many or all of the so-called sightings are hoaxes. But the claimed encounter by Granny's grandfather with *something* in the forest happened more than 100 years ago. Because of the total isolation of the village in his time, it's impossible that he could have heard of Bigfoot and I doubt if he had the imagination to invent what he claimed to have seen. He had no reason to anyway. My granny also wouldn't have heard of Bigfoot and had no reason to make up the story. It's also very strange that her grandfather's description of the creature seems quite close to what others have claimed to have seen in more recent times.

Some cryptozoologists believe that Bigfoot and the Yeti are descendants of Gigantopithecus, a three-metre-tall ape which is known to have roamed in the forests throughout Southeast Asia. The ape became extinct about 300,000 years ago. Or did it?

Strange and inexplicable happenings seemed to be quite common in my village. When I was about seven years old, a neighbour's son, who was about twenty, was coming home from the paddy fields one late afternoon when he desperately needed to urinate. No Thai farmer would ever urinate on the crops or in the fields, on an old tree or anywhere else that a spirit might reside, but a simple bush or something similar was considered safe. The young man urinated on what he thought was a mound of earth covered in vines. That evening, his penis became horribly and unnaturally swollen and very, very painful. His concerned father questioned him about what he had done that day. When the son told his father about urinating on the mound of earth, he went to check the area. He pulled away the vines and discovered that buried beneath the mound of earth was a very old spirit shrine, lying on its side. He concluded that the area must at one time have been the site of someone's home, though it would have been a very long time ago. The spirit which was presumably still residing in the shrine was understandably upset by being urinated on and had taken its revenge in a suitable way. The father re-erected the shrine and cleaned it up, then told his son to take a plate of offerings and incense to the shrine and beg forgiveness from the spirit. His son did so and his embarrassing little problem cleared up almost immediately.

Oddly enough, a year before that incident a village friend of mine had a strange experience in exactly the same spot. A group of us had gone to the place one evening to forage for a particular edible bug that eats the leaves of tamarind trees. There were two such trees growing close to each other on the piece of land. To get the bugs, we would lay a bamboo mat on the ground beneath a tree, then one of us would climb up and shake the branches, so the bugs fell down on to the mat and could then be collected in a lidded basket. On that occasion my friend climbed the tree. Usually it took about twenty minutes of shaking before we had enough bugs but my friend was up in the tree for only a few minutes before he quickly came down, looking very pale. He said he wanted to go home, but didn't immediately say why in case he scared the rest of us.

When we got back to the village, he told us that while he was in the tree he heard a girl's voice calling to him by name from the other tree, inviting him to climb up to her because the bugs were more plentiful in her tree. When he looked across, he saw a vague white shape that resembled a small child, beckoning to him. It frightened him very much. When I told Granny about this, she remembered that when she was very young there had been an old wooden house on that spot, but a child had died in the house. For years after the death the family had nothing but bad luck. They decided to demolish the house and move away. Eventually, the spirit shrine became covered with dirt and vines and was forgotten.

In Thailand, there's hardly a house, office block, municipal building, hotel, shopping mall, restaurant, bar or even military base that doesn't have a carefully and strategically placed spirit shrine (or spirit house) outside, mounted on a pedestal. Traditionally, Thai people believe that every area of land has its own spirit, *Phra Phum*, so if a building is erected on the land the spirit is, in effect, evicted. To avoid unpleasant repercussions, the owner of the new building installs a miniature house nearby for the spirit to live in and makes regular offerings of food, water, incense, flowers and other gifts to keep the spirit happy. The owner may also ask favours from the spirit for good luck, health or prosperity, and vows to make suitable gifts if the requests are granted.

In traditional Thai belief, there are nine major guardian or protector spirits that need to be pleased, placated or at least not offended; the spirit of the land surrounding the house, of the house or building itself, of the homes of newlyweds, of orchards and farms, of grain stores and barns, of waterways, of animal enclosures, of temples, and of gates, military forts and camps. Each guardian may have a spirit house erected to it, but shrines to the spirit of the land are those most commonly seen.

Spirit houses outside important buildings are often huge and ornate and may even be decorated with fairy lights. Inside there may be a small figurine representing the spirit, as well as of people acting as its servants, with elephants and horses for its convenience, dancers for its entertainment and miniature furniture for its comfort. These days there might even be a model of a television or car, but anything which keeps the spirit happy seems to be acceptable. The Phra Phum figure may sometimes be holding a double-edged sword in its right hand, which it uses to overcome malevolent ghosts on the property. In its left hand the image may be holding a book in which to record notable events occurring on the property, though in modern times (more concerned with accumulating wealth) the book may be replaced with a money bag. Outside on the spirit house balcony will be space for the daily offerings. Private homes have much smaller and simpler versions, often with few internal fixtures, though they are usually still very beautiful. Originally, spirit houses were made of wood and were representations of traditional Thai wooden houses, but now most are made of brightly painted concrete and resemble miniature temples.

Some buildings or homes may have two spirit houses, standing next to each other but with one on a slightly shorter post. One is for the guardian spirit of the land and the other for the guardian spirit of the building itself. The most well known shrine of this type is outside the Erawan Hotel in Bangkok.[11]

Whether it's in the garden of an ordinary home or in the grounds of an important building, the spirit house can't be placed just anywhere. To be effective and to keep the spirit happy, the site must be carefully chosen. For important spirit houses, a Brahmin priest or specialist may be called in to select the site and to decide the most auspicious date for erecting the spirit's new residence, even referring to the land-owner's astrological chart. Ordinary Thai people can't generally afford professional advice but usually know how to site the shrine in the traditional way. The best location is in front of a tree and facing towards the north or northeast. The shrine shouldn't be placed on the left side of a doorway, nor facing a toilet or road. Ideally, the shadow of the building on the property should never fall on the spirit house and vice versa. Once the location has been chosen and the spirit house erected, the priest or specialist will perform a ritual to invite the spirit to take up residence.

Granny's and my parent's houses both had their own spirit shrines. They were little more than undecorated wooden platforms, with the spirit houses themselves made from large, square tin cans with one side cut away. The shrine outside my parent's house was set on a simple wooden pedestal but Granny's stood on top of a small termite mound, which she thought was better than a post. Every morning, Granny and my mother would place offerings of rice, water, incense and flowers on the platforms, while murmuring short prayers to the spirits asking them to keep the family and the land safe. Most houses in the village had similar very basic shrines but for a simple rural spirit, and simple rural people, that was considered sufficient. We didn't have the money for anything grander anyway. The villagers also placed spirit houses in their fields for the guardian spirit of their area of paddy. In her field, Granny chose a tall termite mound as the base of her spirit house because that gave the spirit a nice view over the paddies.

In the garden of my city home I have a little spirit house. It's new but it's in the style of a traditional Thai wooden house and made from very old teak. I hope the guardian spirit of my land enjoys living there. At least once a week, or when I remember, I leave offerings of rice and water in the shrine. My garden attracts many birds and every morning a group of several squirrels visits to eat the fruit or bark from my mango tree. The odd thing is that

Strange half true — I've never seen a bird take the food from a spirit house — or animal

both during my time in the village, and now in the city, I have never once seen a bird, squirrel, rat or anything else take food from a spirit house. I've mentioned this to dozens of people and they all say the same: animals *never* take the food. Isn't that a little strange?

Besides being careful not to upset the guardian spirit of the land, it's also traditionally necessary to placate the spirit of the building itself, before the new building is erected. Some house owners may have a second spirit shrine in their garden for this, but will usually also perform a complex ceremony when the first supporting post of the new building is put into the ground. In its full form the ceremony for erecting the first post *(sao ek)* has many different stages, few of which are actually understood by anybody anymore. The full ceremony is a mix of Brahmanism, Buddhism and animism and has developed over many centuries. For important buildings, it involves Brahmin priests and Buddhist monks, as well as a handful of virgins, with cowry shells to blow and gongs to bang and offerings of gold, silver and holy water to be made. That's nothing at all like the ceremony held when Granny built her new house, but simple rural folk like their ceremonies simple too. The village ceremony I saw had no religious overtones at all and I suspect it was almost entirely animist in origin. Even the monks from the village monastery weren't invited to take part and the only active participant was one of the village elders, who knew the local tradition.

When Granny was first married, my grandfather built a wooden house for them to live in. It was standard rural style; a large one-room house built on about twelve wooden posts about three metres high, with broad wooden steps to reach the living accommodation, and with a thatched roof. All the wood and other materials were collected by Grandfather in the forest and the supporting posts were made from trees that he cut himself. They wouldn't have been big old trees because that sort of strength wasn't necessary for the house and, anyway, rural people don't like to cut old trees. Many years after my grandfather died, some of the supporting posts had become infested with termites and were in poor condition. Granny decided that they needed to be replaced. That meant dismantling the house and rebuilding it on top of the new posts, but with a simple wooden dwelling and lots of helping hands from neighbours, that wasn't a difficult task.

The old house was dismantled but before it could be re-erected on its new supporting posts, a village elder was called in to advise and to perform the ceremony of blessing the sao-ek. Unlike in the full Brahmin ceremony for a new house, the elder didn't need to forecast the most auspicious month, date or time, nor which of the supporting posts would be the sao-ek, nor even where it should be positioned. Granny's new house was to be built on exactly the same site as the old one, so the best site for the new sao-ek was already known: in exactly the same place as that for the old house. Although there was no forecasting of the best date, the ceremony would not have been performed on a Tuesday, Saturday or Sunday since those days are considered unlucky for anything concerning a new house building. Granny didn't want any trees cut to make the new supporting posts so her son made concrete ones himself, building them upright in their foundation holes, using a simple framework of wooden planks and pouring the cement in. Villagers always help each other out in these tasks, so a group of the men assembled to start the rebuilding. Before that, the blessing ceremony had to be held and the guardian spirit invited into the new sao-ek.

The village elder had asked that a selection of offerings be made ready for the ceremony. They included a bunch of sugar cane, the stem of a banana tree, betel leaf, areca nut, tobacco, incense, candles and sticky rice and other ordinary foods wrapped in banana leaves. These were all everyday items in our lives, but for the villagers the house was an everyday place and the house-spirit was a simple rural one, which didn't need offerings of gold and silver or the assistance of virgins. The offerings were tied to the upright sao-ek with white and red sai sin string, and then additional huge bunches of sai sin were tied to the post. Small branches of several trees were also tied on. Traditionally, there are nine auspicious trees which should be grown near a house.[12] In the full Brahmin sao-ek ceremony, branches of each of these trees would be placed in the ground along with the sao-ek. Some of the auspicious trees weren't common to my province, but we did the best we could with those few which were.

While the elder was tying the various offerings to the sao-ek and murmuring charms and blessings, the village workmen sat quietly in a circle around the edge of the site, their hands held respectfully together in a wai, but otherwise not participating. Granny sat in their centre on a stool, keeping a sharp eye on the village elder to make sure he did it right. After the offerings had all been tied to the post, the elder chanted for a while in Pali, the language of the Buddhist scriptures, and then let out several loud cries to attract the spirit to the site, before finally blowing magic spells onto the post. That evening all the members of the family, the work team and the village elder sat around in the centre of the site, surrounded by the upright posts, eating, drinking and creating a happy atmosphere. Rebuilding started the next day and just a week later Granny moved into her new house.

Years afterwards, on one of my return visits to the village, I took a sentimental look at the area where Granny's house used to stand and where I spent so many happy days of my childhood. The house had been demolished by one of her sons after she died and there is nothing remaining now except for the supporting posts.

Spirits sometimes make their homes in the most extraordinary places, not just in spirit houses, shrines or house posts. As a child, I was once trying to catch small fish in a paddy field when a blindingly obvious question occurred to me: *where did the fish come from?* Although there was a canal not far away, our family fields were flooded only by natural rainfall, so how did the fish get there? I asked Granny. She laughed and told me a story that *her* grandmother had told her when she was a little girl, when she had asked exactly the same question.

In paddy fields there are often very old termite mounds, sometimes as big as haystacks. Some may have been long-abandoned by the termites but the mounds remain so strong that their mud walls, mixed with chewed wood and other materials, are as hard as concrete. The central core of some mounds may be a large old tree stump and even when the paddy fields are flooded, the mounds are almost immune to water damage. Although termites are pests, old-time farmers never destroyed the mounds. Instead, when ploughing or planting the paddies, they simply worked around them. Farmers didn't dare damage them because large termite mounds were believed to be the homes of *Nak*: mythical serpent spirits that appear frequently in Hindu and Buddhist legends, as well as in ancient animist tales. Amongst other things, the Nak protect rivers, lakes and waterways.

According to Granny's granny, when a Nak residing in a

termite mound sees that the water in the paddy fields is being drained off, just before the rice is harvested, it will give an earth-shattering hiss that causes the ground to split open. The fish, struggling in the shallow water, fall into the crevice. The Nak hisses again and the ground closes up, trapping the water and the fish inside. In the following year, when the rains start to fall again and the paddies flood, the Nak causes the ground to open so the fish can escape. Even my granny was a bit skeptical about this explanation, but she did remind me that some creatures, like frogs, are able to stay buried underground in a state similar to hibernation, without food or water for considerable periods. But the question remains: if the Nak don't really bury the fish, *where do they come from?*

Sadly, during a return visit to my village, many years after I originally left, I took a walk through the paddy fields and noticed that one of the largest of all the termite mounds of my childhood had gone—destroyed by a tractor.

Although most spirits may prefer to live in grand structures like the Erawan Shrine, or in big old trees, spooky groves and termite mounds, some can be enticed into even very small objects, if suitable rituals are performed. Granny once sent me on an errand to a neighbour's house, one I had never been inside before. While I was there, I noticed a curious, brightly painted, small clay image of a child on a high shelf, surrounded by candles, food and, oddly, little toys, including a car. When I got home I asked Granny about the image. She was quite dismissive about it and said that particular image wasn't a powerful one because it hadn't been made by a famous sorcerer-monk. Granny said the image was named *Kuman Thong* and represented the spirit or ghost of a beautiful boy-child. She only knew the basic story, without many of the details which I later discovered for myself.

In the Ayutthaya period of Thai history, between 1350 and 1756, a soldier named Khun Phaen wanted a protective spirit to help him in his battles. One of his minor wives had recently died while pregnant. When pregnant women and their unborn babies died together, they would often be buried rather than cremated. One night, Khun Phaen dug up his wife's corpse and removed the fetus of his unborn son. Fearing that the ghost of his dead wife would try to stop him, he hurried to the consecrated area of a monastery, which ghosts cannot enter. Once there, he prepared magical equipment for the ritual, including candles, metal tablets inscribed with mystic symbols, and images of various ancient gods. He built a small fire using very old wood with magical properties, wrapped the fetus in a cloth and then very slowly and carefully baked it for many hours, while chanting mantras and magic spells. At the end of the baking and chanting, the spirit appeared and Khun Phaen trapped it in a small image of a boy-child that he had made. He named it Kuman Thong.

This story—known as *Khun Chang Khun Phaen*—is actually a literary invention in an epic poem by Thailand's great poet Sunthon-Phu (1786–1855) but it started a belief in the power of baby spirits that has lasted nearly two hundred years and seems to be growing stronger all the time. Nowadays, the images are said to bring good luck and prosperity to their owners, provided that Kuman Thong is offered food and drinks every day, as well as the occasional toy. He prefers red fizzy drinks and is very popular with shopkeepers. Modern images are usually mass-produced, large doll-like figures, but the most sought-after are those which were made long ago by a few very powerful monks using wood from old temples, or ivory, bronze or plaster (but not, of course, using real fetuses). The monk chanted over the image, inviting the spirit of a dead baby to take up residence in it. For the monk, providing a home in the image for the baby spirit wasn't about black magic; it was an act of compassion, since otherwise the spirit would wander aimlessly forever. The spirit, grateful for its new home, would in return bring prosperity to the image owner. Old images made by a renowned past master and believed to contain a baby spirit can be very valuable and are thought to be very powerful.

Literary invention or not, there was a slightly spooky aspect to the Kuman Thong image that I saw in the village house. Although Granny had scornfully dismissed the image as being not very powerful, neighbours often reported hearing a little boy running about and laughing in that house, though the couple who lived there had no children.

Granny had an important image of her own. She once showed me a very old, tiny, lacquered bamboo image of a buffalo, though she wouldn't let me touch it. The image had belonged to my grandfather and perhaps even to *his* grandfather. It was no more than about four centimetres long and was so heavily lacquered that it was quite difficult to make out what it represented. Granny said the image was very powerful, having been made long ago by a sorcerer.

In many houses in my village, and all over rural Thailand, there can still sometimes be seen such images of a cow or buffalo, called *Wua Thanu* or *Khwai Thanu*, set on a high shelf, though the images are rarely old ones. Most old-time farmers keep them simply in the belief that they will help protect and bring prosperity to the land, and they may make offerings of fresh grass and water to the image every day.

Older images have a darker side and have become associated with black magic rituals. Traditionally, the most powerful images for use in magic were made only from very specific materials, including seven nails from seven different coffins, metal from the roof of a ruined monastery pagoda, lacquered bamboo, copper, wax, or from a collection of particular dried and powdered flowers mixed with clay taken from a cemetery. After being made, a sorcerer would chant over the image and cast a spell, causing the image to become actively powerful. Sometimes, a magic spell written on parchment or metal would be concealed within the base of the image. Granny told me that although modern Khwai Thanu images are intended to be only beneficial, very old ones can be used to cause harm to one's enemies. By holding the image tightly in the hand while thinking bad thoughts about a particular person, that person will suffer great misfortune.

After Granny died her Khwai Thanu image could not be found in her house. Many years later, a very old lady in the village told me that if a powerful Khwai Thanu is not passed on personally by its owner to a new owner, the image will simply vanish on the next full moon night and go searching for a new owner by itself. It was assumed that Granny's image had done that.

Many strange things seem to happen on full moon nights. One evening, on a full moon night, my family and neighbours were sitting chatting outside Granny's house when she glanced up at the sky and suddenly shouted: *dok! dok! dok!* All the adults immediately jumped up and ran frantically towards the nearest big trees, where they started knocking on the trunks and calling out *dok! dok! dok!* over and over again. As they knocked on the trees, the men patted their pockets, while some of the women rubbed their stomachs. This was very strange behavior, even for my village. Granny couldn't walk very well but she was obviously desperate to have a knock and a pat too, so she told me to run to a particular big guava tree, knock on it and go through the *dok, dok, dok* routine. I did, and then asked what it was all about. It was quite hard to hear what Granny was saying because our conversation was constantly interrupted by village men shooting their muskets at the moon. It was only then that I saw that the moon seemed to have a piece missing. It was a lunar eclipse.

I doubt if anybody in the village knew what a lunar or solar eclipse was or would have been able to explain them scientifically, or even in the simplest layman's terms. Any eclipse was a strange, unexpected and portentous event, but Granny usually had some ancient myth to account for such things. She told me that the men were shooting their guns at the moon because a sky god was trying to eat it. That didn't explain the tree-knocking or *dok* business, but I was only about eight years old then and I think Granny blurred the story a little. Many years later, long after Granny had passed away, I asked an uncle about the myth and he laughed and said, *no*, the sky god wasn't *eating* the moon, it was having *sex* with the moon goddess. The myth began to make more sense. 'Dok' in the ancient Khammueang language means 'plentiful'. When the gods have sex, that's a good time for wishing on an old tree for a good harvest, or more fruit on the trees, or for anything to be more plentiful, including the money in your pocket or babies in the womb; hence the men's pocket tapping and the women's belly rubbing.

Not all Thai superstitions or traditions are concerned with spirits, ghosts or ancient myths. Some have a practical basis. Granny would often tell me: *Don't do that, it's unlucky*. My response would usually be: *Why?* She would then tell me to think about it and try and discover the reason for myself. The origins of some superstitions were obvious but others were more obscure.

One of my chores as a child was to sweep Granny's floor and to brush away spider webs from the ceiling and corners, but she told me not to do either at night because it was unlucky. Why was it unlucky? Because our houses didn't have electricity and were lit only by a couple of kerosene lamps, so the house was quite dark at night. It was wise not to sweep the floor in the dark in case small coins or valuables might have been dropped during the day, though that was unlikely because we didn't have any. The coins might be accidentally swept out of the house and lost. Small snakes could also be lurking in the dark corners of the house and might attack if the broom brushed against them. It was unlucky to sweep cobwebs off the ceiling at night because wooden houses attract lots of spiders and they can spin their webs in a few hours. Even some very small spiders in Thailand can give a nasty bite, so it would definitely be unlucky to sweep a web off the ceiling and have an angry venomous spider drop on your head.

I remember one time when somebody in the village died and Granny wouldn't let me go to the funeral. She said it would be unlucky because at that time I had a new graze on my elbow. Because there was a death involved, I assumed that must have been connected somehow with ghosts or spirits, but I later discovered that it was for a more practical and sensible reason. Sometimes in the village, when somebody died unexpectedly from something other than old age or an obvious accident, we might not know the cause of death. At that time the village was very isolated and few people had transport, so the sick weren't easily able to visit a city doctor or hospital and there were no autopsies on those who died, nor even death certificates. Thai people are very pragmatic about death and at funerals the coffin is usually left open, so mourners can lay incense sticks on the corpse before it's cremated. If a mourner has an open wound and gets close to the coffin, the wound could be infected by bacteria from the corpse or by a disease that might have killed the dead person. Quite a sensible and obvious basic health precaution, wrapped up in a superstition.

Less obvious are some others which I have heard about. Never—*never*—have your haircut on a Wednesday. Nothing but bad luck will follow for the rest of the day. Any other day is fine and will bring good luck or prosperity of one kind or another. Monday will bring good health, Tuesday will bring power, Thursday is a good day for taking a risk because your guardian spirit will protect you, on Friday you will not want for anything, on Saturday people will admire your every action and compliment you and on Sunday you will have a long life. That doesn't explain why Wednesday is an *un*lucky day, but I suppose there was nothing good left to say. Having my haircut on any particular day never concerned me. Like most of the other boys in the village, my head was regularly shaved by Granny for the early years of my life, after which I was a head-shaven novice monk for seven years, so I never visited a professional hairdresser until I was about eighteen years old. I do recall that when I went to have my very first haircut in a little up-country shop, the hairdresser was closed because it was a Wednesday, so I couldn't get it cut that day. Lucky for me!

There are other superstitions and traditions associated with hair. In my village, any newborn baby usually had its head carefully shaved for the first several months of its life, in the belief that the hair would eventually grow thicker and stronger. A baby or toddler who cried a lot would have its head shaved except for one hair. After a couple of months, that single hair would also be shaved off, after which it was believed the child wouldn't cry so frequently. Rarely seen nowadays except in very remote areas is the full topknot. It's an ancient belief that a preteen child who is often sick, or even accident prone, can be cured by shaving the head except for a topknot. The topknot might be grown for several years, with the rest of the hair being shaved off regularly, until the child is as much as thirteen years old. The topknot is eventually cut off in a tonsure ceremony, sometimes performed by a Buddhist monk.

It was also a common belief that it was unlucky to tap a baby on the head. It was thought that tapping on the head could frighten the baby's young khwan; the spirit or 'soul' that resides there. Frightening the khwan could cause the child to wet the bed often. That's really quite a sensible superstition because a baby's skull is not yet hard or fully developed, so tapping it could cause damage. All new babies in the village, including me, had their shaved heads covered with a mixture of turmeric and other herbs. The mixture was allowed to form into a semi-hard dry lump several centimetres across in the middle of the baby's head. It was washed off and replaced every day until the baby seemed strong and healthy. It looked very strange but was intended to protect that part of the head while it was still being formed and hardened and was also believed to protect against colds and baby illnesses.

On the ghostly side, if you meet a Thai mother with her new baby, it really isn't a good idea to exclaim: *What a beautiful baby!* The mother might be quite upset. If you loudly mention how beautiful or cute the baby is, your comment might attract the attention of a passing ghost who could then take an interest in the child and even possess it. But *What an little ugly monster!*

very different to the west

might also cause offence to the mother, so it's probably wisest not to say anything at all. In this difficult no-win situation, Thai people usually say *narak nachang*, which means something like: *lovable, but ugly too.* All Thai's seem to use their nicknames

Newborn babies in Thailand are usually given a nickname at birth, as well as an official name. That's to confuse any ghosts that may be lurking around, because to know the child's real name could give a malevolent wandering spirit control over him or her. Although the real name isn't a secret, a person might use his or her birth nickname throughout their life and even close acquaintances or workplace colleagues may never know or even think to ask the real name. The nickname may simply be a shortened version of the official name; my full name is *Sorasing*—which means something like *roar of a lion*—and my nickname is *Sing*. Some babies may be given a nickname by their parents which to a Westerner might seem rather unkind; *Mu* (pig) is quite a common one, so is *Uan* (fat) but neither is considered in the least bit impolite by Thai people, nor embarrassing for the person who goes by that name. Other parents may give their newborn a nickname which has no particular meaning but is given simply because they like the sound of the word.

Knocking over a bowl of rice is considered very unlucky and something bad will happen that day. In the superstition that's obviously because Mae Phosop, the Rice Mother, can get a bit touchy if her grains are abused, but it also simply makes children more careful in their behavior. When eating rice, it's considered unlucky to talk about anything bad that happened in the day, or a nightmare you had the previous night. Mae Phosop is very sensitive and doesn't want to hear about unpleasant things while people are eating her grains, but I suppose talking about such things can also cause people simply to lose their appetite, which is not polite.

Possibly one of the oddest superstitions I've heard is that a woman shouldn't bend over and look between her legs. If she does she will see a ghost standing behind her. I can't think why any woman should want to do that, but the explanation is that in former times village women sometimes didn't wear underwear, just their wrap-around sarongs. If they stood up, bent over and looked between their spread legs—causing their sarongs to fall open—they might see a ghost, but other people might see more than that, which wouldn't be polite.

There are also many superstitions attached to animals. In my village, when we heard a tukkae make its loud bark-like sound, we would count the number of times it called. If it called an even number of times, that was lucky, but if it called an uneven number of times something bad could happen that day. It was also believed that the tukkae's little cousin, the jing-jok, could also foretell the immediate future. If one made its *tch! tch!* cry just as we were leaving the house, it was best to wait a while before going out. And if one fell on your head as you were leaving the house, better not to go out at all.

At the other end of the size scale, there was a common superstition in the village about elephants. When I was a child at primary school I learned about elephants but I didn't see one until I was about eight years old. It passed Granny's house with its mahout on their way to a logging camp in another province. I was very frightened of the huge beast and Granny and my mother warned me not to follow it and especially not to tread in its footprints. It was believed in the village then that doing so could lead to elephantiasis; a huge swelling of the feet and legs.[13] It was also considered very unlucky for a pregnant woman to go anywhere near an elephant because that might lead to a miscarriage. That's strange because in modern times in the cities, expectant mothers will pay a mahout for the privilege of walking beneath the belly of his elephant, believing it to be lucky. Obviously, what was considered an unlucky superstition at one time and in one place can have quite a different interpretation in another time and place.

'If We Can't Make It, We Don't Need It'

In the village, there were very few things in our lives that weren't handmade, either by someone in the family itself or by some other local skilled craftsman. We were almost totally self-sufficient and we were natural recyclers. Granny often said: "*If we can't make it, we don't need it*" and that was usually true. Just about the only thing we couldn't create ourselves from scratch was anything which had to be cast from metal. There was no smelting works, forge or metal-making skill in the village so tools like sickles, hoes, saws, hammers, chisels, axes, knives or cooking pots all had to be bought in the city or from travelling salesmen who occasionally passed through the village. But even those metal things rarely had to be bought new.

My grandfather's axe and other woodworking tools which he used to build his house had been in his family for generations, and Granny's heavy iron cooking pots and pans had been in her family for just as long. When I look back to my childhood days and picture the few metal things that we used, I realise now that most of them must have been *hundreds* of years old; an antique dealer's dream. Even the nails that held Granny's house together were recycled by Grandfather from the ruins of an abandoned old house in the village, so they were probably getting on for a century old. Any old bent nail found anywhere would be carefully straightened out and hoarded. If Grandfather hadn't been able to recycle metal nails, he would probably have made wooden dowel pins, as his forefathers had done. My grandfather's wood-working tools are still in use by my uncle, who built his own new wooden house with them. Most of Granny's cooking pots are also still in use, and still going strong. Metal was not a big part of our lives then but what we had was used for generations and was always recyclable.

Almost everything was recycled. Something had to be *totally* worn out and unsuitable for its original purpose before it was discarded, but even then it could usually be transformed into something else. The snapped blade of an ancient kitchen knife might become the cutting edge of a homemade wooden-handled chisel, or simply ground down on a stone to make a shorter knife. Even a shard of a broken glass bottle would make a decent chisel or plane. A large tin can could make a respectable spirit house and my uncle once made a Stone Age-type hammer from a broken granite pestle, with the stone bound with twine to a wooden handle. After Granny's time, when worn-out car tyres were sometimes available in the village, they could be cut up and made into rubber flip-flop sandals. Some things could be recycled many times over several years before their usefulness was ended. I remember an old, out-grown school shirt of mine that Granny first recycled into a washcloth, then later into a foot mat, then into clothes for a scarecrow and which was finally shredded up with other old clothes, mixed with rice husks and clay and used to make crude bricks for the walls of a charcoal kiln.

Granny never threw anything away and rarely had to buy anything, but village folk then were nothing like modern consumers, dashing out shopping every five minutes to acquire something new. There was no local shop and to get to the nearest city store was a ten-hour round trip. There wasn't much of a cash economy in the community but villagers wouldn't have known what to buy anyway. The ordinary things that surrounded us in our daily lives were the only things we knew of. Because we didn't have televisions, radios, newspapers or magazines in the village until the late 1980s, we had no idea what else was available in the big, wide world beyond the borders of our isolated community and we weren't constantly bombarded with advertisements to buy new products. Granny would never have looked at her ancient iron wok and wistfully dreamed that she had a stainless-steel one coated with non-stick Teflon; she couldn't have imagined such things existed and was very happy with what she did have. Much of her cookware was handmade by her from clay which she claimed—quite rightly—gave a much better flavour to some 'hot pot' foods when they were cooked very slowly over a charcoal brazier. Both the brazier and the charcoal itself were also homemade in Granny's kiln.

My grandfather built a brick charcoal kiln after he and Granny were married. Though often repaired, the kiln was still very usable many years after he died. Granny's kiln was dome-shaped, something like an igloo, with three flue holes at the top and a semi-circular entrance at the base. Although the kiln was only about a metre and a half tall, the earth inside had been dug out, making it deeper. Granny collected dead wood in the forest to make her charcoal, but even that required a knowledge of folklore. Some wood made charcoal which burned hotter than others, some wood was considered unlucky to have near the house and some wasn't used because its charcoal burned with too much flame or spark. After being loaded wigwam-shape into the kiln, the logs were allowed to burn freely for a day or so and then the kiln entrance and flues were blocked with bricks, leaving the wood to smolder for several more days. The kiln was almost constantly burning. If I was out foraging for food and didn't catch anything, I was at least expected to return with an armful of suitable wood.

Abandoned termite mounds also make very efficient charcoal kilns when hollowed out, since their side walls are often as solid as brick. In my childhood days, there were hundreds, probably thousands, of small mounds, a metre or so tall, in and around the village. Every house seemed to have at least one on the property. There were also a few huge ones in the paddy fields. The very large ones were considered to be the homes of spirits and were treated with great respect and never damaged, but the smaller mounds were sometimes turned into kilns, though Granny was usually consulted first, just to be on the safe side. She would sometimes recommend that a little spirit house be erected near to the mound, for any displaced spirit to live in. Granny had a small termite mound in front of her house and though she wouldn't consider using it as a kiln, she had sat a spirit house on top of it.

These days only a few families in the village still make their own charcoal and most cook on bottled gas, though I do know of one remaining and still operating termite mound kiln which has been in use by the same family for at least fifty years. There are very few mounds in family compounds anymore. People obviously don't want termites near their wooden houses and they usually destroy the mounds and kill the termites, regardless of ancient beliefs.

Making bricks was just one of Granny's many skills. There were few things we used regularly that she couldn't make. Granny handmade most of our household necessities including; cotton, bamboo baskets, animal traps, small items of earthenware, large sheets of woven bamboo to cover walls or ceilings, thick rope, fine twine, fishing nets, sleeping mats, blankets, pillows, brooms, thatch and charcoal. Granny didn't only make small things—she could handweave a large, complex rice-milling machine from bamboo or even weave her own rice store. Despite the calluses from years of hard work in the paddy fields, Granny's fingers remained incredibly nimble until the day she died, but weaving bamboo was her greatest skill.

All Granny's many different bamboo baskets, trays and traps were woven to centuries-old traditional designs, but there were no patterns or examples to follow; she simply remembered what she had learned as a child from watching her mother and grandmother. She would never consider making even the simplest change to any of the designs and her work was always precise. If two of her baskets of the same type were put side by side, it would be near impossible to tell them apart. They were exactly the same in every tiny and intricate detail, as though mass-produced on a machine. Once, when I was watching her weave a basket with a pentagonal base, used specifically to make seasonal offerings to Mae Phosop, the Rice Mother, I innocently suggested that it would be easier if the base was square. She was rather shocked at the idea of such radical change to centuries-old tradition and said *no*, it *must* have five angles, though she couldn't explain why. I've since learned that each angle represented one of five Hindu gods.

I often sat with Granny while she wove bamboo, but I didn't appreciate then just how remarkably skilled she was. Bamboo baskets were everyday, common things to me. It wasn't until years after Granny died, when I started to become interested in rural

169

handicrafts, that I fully realised not only the skill but also the *art* that went into everything she made. By changing the width, thickness, placement or angle of the bamboo, she could produce complex patterns, shades and textures in her finished work that turned the simplest and most utilitarian item into something quite beautiful. Her baskets, trays and traps were all made to serve some simple everyday purpose—like sieving rice or catching a fish—and they didn't *need* to be so intricate or so beautiful; it was simply the way things were done, and had always been done.

There are hundreds of species of bamboo and several grew in the forests around the village. Granny told me that different species were more, or less, suitable for various types of basketry and had different colouration, but she often used a yellow bamboo known locally as *Phai Sisuk*. The age of the individual bamboo stem used was also very important and Granny chose her material with great care, depending on what she wanted to make. She would never use any stem that was not perfectly straight or was scratched, bruised, burned or which showed signs of insect damage. She cut some stems when they were just a few months old, for softness and flexibility, while others might be several years old, for thickness and strength. She never cut any stem that was more than about four years old, because by that time fungus and mould had usually started to attack the plant, causing internal damage to the stems and making them unsuitable for most types of weaving.

Granny used only two simple tools in all her bamboo work; a machete for cutting the stems from the parent plant and a small, very sharp knife for shaving the cut stems into thin strips of many different thicknesses and widths, depending on what she planned to make. After the strips had dried in the sun for a day or two, she could weave baskets and traps of dozens of sizes and uses; traps for catching fish, eels, rats, mice, snakes, small birds and even insects, and they all worked very well. Her many varieties of basket even included a bucket-shaped one that she heavily coated with an insect-produced lacquer, for carrying water. I've since seen baskets and traps of exactly the same kinds in a museum of traditional but largely lost rural handicrafts.

Depending on their purpose, some baskets and traps were woven so tightly that they were almost as strong and as solid as if they had been carved from wood, while others were as soft and flexible as cloth. Making any basket was a time-consuming task and particularly intricate ones could take up to a week to complete. When they were finished, Granny would hang them from the beams under the house for several months to absorb charcoal smoke, which strengthened the bamboo and gave it a beautiful mahogany colour. Some traps for catching fish, eels or frogs were made to be immersed in water, but the smoke helped waterproof the bamboo and also deterred insects and rodents from attacking it.

Granny learned her basket making skills from her mother. Unfortunately, both Granny and my own mother died before they could pass on their skills to me, but Granny taught her son to weave bamboo in the traditional way. I have a basket that he made to one of Granny's designs. It's a simple, everyday thing for carrying freshly caught fish from the canal back to the house, yet it is elegant, sturdy and quite beautiful. It looks a little like a classical Greek urn, oval and slightly bulbous in shape. It's about fifteen centimetres across at the base, thirty centimetres across at the shoulders and thirty centimetres high. The square base is an x-shape of two wide pieces of bamboo which support nearly fifty vertical spokes. Woven horizontally very closely through the spokes to the height of the shoulders are fifty narrow strips, followed by ten broader loosely woven strips, allowing air into the basket, which are placed at a different angle to the main body. The shaped neck of the basket is made from twenty closely woven narrow strips, culminating in a thick rim bound with twine. The basket has two loops at the shoulders for a carrying string and a tightly fitting, escape-proof conical lid. The basket has been hardened and deeply coloured by charcoal smoke. It took several evenings to make and it is, quite simply, a work of art—and it was made for carrying fish.

My uncle's teenage son has no interest in traditional handicrafts and can't weave even the simplest basket. Like many of his young village friends, he's studying electronics at college and plans to move away from home as soon as possible to work in a city. Basket weaving is a skill which will probably be entirely lost in the village within a generation or two.

Weaving cotton was another of Granny's great skills. Unlike in the upper northern and northeastern provinces, silk weaving wasn't a known craft in my village, I think because of the poor quality or unavailability of mulberry leaves on which the silk worms feed. Instead, the women spun and weaved cotton on homemade wooden floor looms, with cotton bolls gathered from local uncultivated trees. Granny's very large and complex loom stood in the space beneath her house. As a child, the loom seemed rather intimidating to me but I was not allowed near it anyway. The only job Granny allowed me to do was to pick out the little black seeds from the dried cotton bolls, before the cotton fibres were fluffed up and carded. I always very much enjoyed watching Granny spin the cotton into yarn on her ancient spinning wheel and longed to try it myself. Granny promised to teach me the craft, but we somehow never got around to it.

Most of our family clothes were made on the loom in traditional designs and colours; designs that hadn't changed for hundreds of years. Besides weaving all the cloth herself, Granny also made her own dyes which she distilled from flowers, leaves, seeds, tree bark and roots. Granny knew how to produce almost any colour imaginable, though the traditional cloth designs that she made didn't require a wide variety of shades; mango root for black, hog plum leaves for green, blue from the leaves and stems of the indigo shrub, an insect-secreted resin for red and jackfruit core for yellow: the same yellow dye used thousands of years ago in the Buddha's time when monks made their own robes. Dying the cloth was an art in itself and sometimes involved hours of soaking the ingredients, then boiling, decanting and filtering the liquid, before the plain cotton was added.

Granny's cotton loom had been passed down from mother to daughter for generations and was certainly more than a hundred years old. When I was a boy there were several such looms in the village, but after Granny died in 1991 one of her children sold Granny's loom to a Bangkok antique dealer for the princely sum of two hundred baht. That was a fortune for villagers in those days and when the other women heard about it, they were quick to sell their own looms too. There are no looms in the village anymore and the weaving skills have been entirely lost. Villagers now buy their clothes in the city.

Although I later came to appreciate Granny's basketry and cloth-weaving artistry, at the time I was much more impressed by her toy-making skills. She made all my childhood toys. They were all very simple of course, made from whatever was to hand, but I certainly had as much fun with them as any modern child, with his expensive electronic or battery-powered toys, games and gadgets. The earliest toy I remember was a hobbyhorse, which Granny made for me when I was about four or five years old. She told me that when she was a little girl, she saw a wild horse in the forest; the first and only time she ever saw a horse. The memory and the image had always stayed with her and she based her horse head design on what she remembered seeing, from all those years ago. My hobbyhorse was virtually the same as Western children played with: a wooden stick to hold between the legs and with a horse's head at one end. Mine was made from a young banana tree stem, with a banana leaf cut to the shape of the head. Granny sometimes made them for all my little friends and, crude though they may have been, our hobbyhorses gave us hours of fun as we rode around the village in a posse. My hobbyhorses never lasted very long, but a new one could be made in minutes.

I also used to have great fun with two half coconut shells, to which Granny would attach long strings. The idea was to walk around on the shells while pulling the strings tight in the hands to keep the shells firmly against the soles of the feet. I would clomp around for hours like that, though I can't think now why it seemed so much fun. When I got a bit older I graduated to stilts, made by Granny from a couple of bamboo poles with pegs to stand on. Later still, she made me a compressed-air gun from two lengths of bamboo fitted tightly one inside the other. It could shoot a hard seed ten metres or more, keeping me amused all day. Granny also made rattan balls for playing the Thai national game of *takraw*[14], banana leaf noise-makers and a dozen other simple, effective toys, all created from everyday things found in our environment. Now of course village children have plastic toys, but in my childhood

I never had anything made of plastic until I was seven years old.

The first plastic thing I ever owned was when my mother bought me a toothbrush as a present for my seventh birthday. She got it from a travelling salesman and it was the first real toothbrush I had ever seen. It cost mother the equivalent of several hours of labouring in the paddy fields. I loved my plastic toothbrush, but Granny just laughed scornfully when she saw it. Like her own grandmother, she'd been brushing her teeth with a chewed twig and rock salt every day since she was a little girl, as rural folk had been doing throughout Southeast Asia for thousands of years. She took me outside the house and pointed to the Khoi tree which supplied her with twigs. '*Look!*' she said. '*A lifetime of toothbrushes. Free! Who needs to spend money to buy a plastic stick to do the same job?*'

Granny would have been a marketing man's worst nightmare.

Something to Celebrate

There wasn't much to celebrate when I was a child in the village. We laboured nearly every day, stopping work usually only for the three days of the Songkran New Year holiday. That was a welcome and happy time in the village; a time of relaxation and renewal, an occasion to come together as a family and as a community and an opportunity to pay our respects to our elders and ancestors. All other national holidays and festivals simply passed us by and there were no celebrations specific to my village, or even to the province. Granny certainly hadn't heard about the ghost festival, mysterious fireballs or any of the other strange events and festivals that went on outside our remote little community.[15]

During my childhood, I made only a few day trips out of the village to Uttaradit City, which was about twenty-five kilometres away. We never saw a newspaper in the village (most people couldn't read) and there were no televisions or radios, so we knew little about what went on in the outside world. Because my early years had been so sheltered, it was something of a shock when I moved to a city as a novice monk and saw for the first time how the beautiful and simple Songkran Festival we celebrated in the village seemed to have degenerated into a rowdy, drunken free-for-all. Granny would have been absolutely horrified. But even though I was a novice monk and couldn't take part in the street parties and wild water throwing, I thought it was great fun. I still think so, for those who want to be involved, but I miss the beauty and simplicity of the traditional Songkran I knew in my childhood.

Songkran is celebrated over three days in the hottest month of the year, from 13 April to 15 April, though in recent times the holiday is usually stretched to a full week. That's good, because Thai families are sometimes very scattered. Whole branches of rural families, perhaps not able to make a living from the land, or individual members not needed by their families to help in the fields, may move to Bangkok or other cities to work as building labourers or in other unskilled, menial jobs. They often work seven days a week and the only time off they usually have each year is at Songkran. Then, almost without exception, they make the long return journey to their home provinces and family villages. Travelling anywhere by car or public transport is a nightmare during the holiday. The entire population of Thailand seems to be on the move and Bangkok becomes an empty ghost city. Regardless of the difficulties of getting home, everybody wants to return to be united with their families and to take part in the celebrations. Although in my village Songkran was celebrated in the traditional and low-key way—the only way we knew—it still meant a few days when we didn't have to work in the fields or, in my case, go to school. We all looked forward to it for weeks beforehand.

On each of the three days of the holiday there are many traditional activities. Some of these are also still celebrated in the cities, but the *why* has sometimes long been forgotten by city-dwellers, especially the young. In my village, we hadn't forgotten and they were very important to all of us, even the children. The activities and ceremonies were taken seriously because they were not only to welcome in the New Year and see out the old, but were also aimed at increasing harmony and unity within the community as a whole, as well as within individual families.

The specific day for each activity can vary from region to region, or even from village to village. In my village, on the day before the official start of the Songkran holiday, I always helped Granny give the house and surrounding area a thorough cleaning, not just because visitors were expected, but to symbolically wash out the old year and welcome in the new. We also gave Granny's small Buddha image a gentle wash with scented water, being very careful and respectful in the way the image was handled. That evening, the older village men would go to the barren rice paddies and sit together in a circle on bamboo mats on this last night of the old year. They would talk over events in the village during the past year and their hopes and plans for the coming year. Marriages between their children in the New Year might be hinted at, deals would be proposed for the exchange of small plots of land and outstanding disputes and animosities would be settled so as not to carry them on into the New Year. They would drink a little of the local rice whisky, but on that occasion not too much. All through their get-together, they would fire their muskets into the air, in the belief that this would invite beneficial spirits to join the coming celebrations. The guns were always aimed towards the South, though unfortunately none of the very old village men that I've talked to can remember why.

On the first morning of the holiday the entire population of the village visited the local monastery to pay respect to the monks. Most of the women were laden down with two bamboo baskets of food, hung from a long pole carried over their shoulders. Everybody wore their best clothes. Our best was usually little better than our everyday working clothes, but it was important to us to be as well turned out as possible throughout Songkran.

The monastery was the heart of our little community. Villagers usually turned to the monks, and particularly the abbot, not only for spiritual advice but also to help solve petty disputes. If relevant, the abbot sometimes discussed these disputes with the village elders, including Granny as matriarch, to get their opinion before he made his decision. More serious issues were also sometimes settled by the abbot, which was considered a better course of action than involving provincial officials or the police, who weren't as well-trusted in those days. We respected all the monks very much. All the longer-term monks had been born in the village or nearby and a few young village men ordained at the monastery each year for the duration of the three months' *Phansa*, or Rains Retreat[16], traditionally to make merit for their parents, as well as to learn more about the teaching of the Buddha.

On the first morning of the holiday, we offered the best food we had to the monks and then, on behalf of our ancestors, made gifts of tobacco, soap and other small everyday items. Listening to the monks' chanting and the abbot's sermon took up most of the morning, but we were all avid listeners. The sermons were often based around the Buddha's teaching about the four great qualities that everybody should try to develop; goodwill towards others, compassion for all creatures, joy at other's success or happiness, and equanimity of mind. It was good that we should be reminded of those qualities at the start of the New Year. The abbot would also intone the five precepts of Buddhist laypeople and we would repeat them, line by line; to refrain from harming any living creature, to refrain from taking what is not given, to refrain from sexual misconduct, to refrain from wrong speech, and to refrain from drink or drugs that cloud the mind.

In the late afternoon, we returned to the monastery carrying bottles or containers of clean water, to which was added fragrant white jasmine and other flower petals. We transferred the water into tiny silver-alloy cups and each villager slowly and carefully poured a little over the main Buddha image, symbolically bathing it. The image was a bronze about one metre tall and was believed to be hundreds of years old. Whilst bathing the image, we each quietly asked forgiveness from the Buddha for our bad actions during the past year and requested blessings for the New Year. Even as a little boy, I always felt a sense of relief when I did that. Granny told me that if I did it sincerely, my boyish mischief and misdeeds of the past year would be washed away.

When villagers died and were cremated, the remains were sometimes sealed inside concrete chedi or pagodas in the monastery grounds. These chedi were often very beautiful, being covered in marble, ceramics or multi-coloured glass mosaic. Some were large family chedi and might contain the remains of several members of the same family, their names inscribed on marble plaques fixed to the outside. Such chedi were expensive and most families couldn't afford them, so then the remains would be kept at home in small brass or tin chedi-shaped containers, always placed on a high shelf with daily offerings of candles and incense. Other people might bury the remains of their relatives under a pho tree in the monastery grounds. After bathing the Buddha image, families which had interred their relatives' remains in the monastery would pour a little scented water over the chedi or onto the roots of the tree where the remains were buried. That wasn't empty ritual; while slowly pouring the water, relatives would quietly pay respect to the memory of the deceased.

Meanwhile the monks had assembled in the grounds for their own ritual bathing. They sat in a line on long wooden benches, their eyes downcast and their hands cupped in their laps. A long queue of villagers walked in front of or behind the monks and each gently poured a little scented water over the monks' shoulders and hands, but never on their heads. The water collected in the monks' hands and they would sometimes flick a little of it over us as a blessing, as we passed by in a line. Although bathing the monks always started off as a serious ceremony, it would quickly degenerate into the opportunity for a little *sanuk* (fun). For the village children especially, soaking the younger monks with a little *too much* water was considered hilarious. The monks' robes were always completely drenched by the end of it but they took their soaking with good humour. They had done exactly the same thing when they were village boys. Their ritual bath finished, the monks chanted a blessing for us, while we sat on straw mats, our heads lowered and our hands held in the prayer-like attitude known as *anchali*.

On the second day we would again go to the monastery to offer breakfast to the monks and to listen to a sermon, and then return in the afternoon with small quantities of clean sand, collected from the river. Granny told me that nothing should ever be taken from a monastery, not even dirt from the grounds, so we had to replace any dirt carried away by our feet during the past year with fresh sand. Mixed with water, the sand was built into small pagodas, much like children's sand castles, and decorated with flags, candles, incense and flowers. In some regions, small coins are also buried within the pagodas but that wasn't common in my village, simply because nobody had any spare money. Building the pagodas could go on for hours, with the village children competing to see who could create the most splendid one. The pagodas were later knocked down and the sand was spread evenly around the monastery grounds. That was also a way to symbolically raise the level of the earth, as a protection against flooding.

There was another much-anticipated ceremony on that day. In the early evening, the villagers would go with the monks to what was considered the geographic centre of the community. The spiritual centre was the monastery but the geographic centre was then a paddy field, though that has since become a road junction. In the field we would make offerings to the spirits of the village, of the fields and forest, and to all the natural elements that were such a part of our environment. That was an important ritual for us. We were a small and close-knit community, relying on each other for support and on the natural environment to sustain us. Harmony within the community and with the environment was essential to our survival. We would all sit on the earth in front of the monks with little square plates made from the stems of a banana tree. On the plates were small, crude clay images of the creatures that lived around us and which played such an important role in our daily lives. Granny had shown me how to make these little animals when I was a child. Representations of buffaloes, oxen, chickens, snakes, birds, fish and many other creatures were placed on the banana plates, together with offerings of sticky rice, incense and candles. Granny and the other village elders would talk to us about the coming year—an annual pep talk—to instill a sense of harmony, community spirit and personal worth within us. Then, while the monks chanted, the plates of offerings would be placed around the field with a silent prayer to the spirits. It gave all of us, even the children, a sense that our duty to the spirits had been properly and duly performed. That night there would usually be a movie show or some other community entertainment in the monastery grounds, which even Granny would attend.

If our ancestors' ashes were kept at home, on the third morning of the holiday we would respectfully carry them with any photographs we had to the monastery for a special blessing called *Bangsakun*. The photographs and miniature chedi containing the ashes would be displayed on a large, high table. After breakfast had been offered to the monks, the photographs and chedi would be wrapped around many times with sai sin string, which then passed through the chanting monks' hands. The sai sin symbolically linked the spirits of the ancestors with the chanting of the Buddha's teaching, which was believed to help our ancestors achieve good future lives. We would again present gifts on behalf of our ancestors, that time including pillows and homemade cotton blankets. Granny was very skilled at making these from a cotton-like fibre gathered in the forest from the kapok tree. Granny always warned me that there could be many ghosts or spirits around on that day, attracted by our activities, and said I had to be very polite and kind to everybody, never use impolite language, not raise my voice or get in an argument with any of my friends. I wasn't even to climb a tree or do anything risky, because that might attract a spirit, which would be a bad beginning to the New Year.

The third day was also the day for paying respect to our living elders. After we got back from the monastery, the entire family would gather at Granny's house for the celebration and a special lunch, which would include pork and, unusually, chicken. Apart from that special day, we rarely killed one of our chickens for food, preferring to keep them only for their eggs.

At Granny's house on that day there could be twenty or thirty people present, many of them having made the long and difficult journey from Bangkok. I wouldn't have seen some of them since the previous Songkran and there were others that I didn't know at all. There were new wives or husbands to be introduced, new babies to be shown off and greetings and gifts to be exchanged. We never spent much time trying to work out how we were related to each other. Thai people are often quite casual about their family relationships, not bothering too much whether somebody is an aunt, uncle, nephew, cousin or whatever, and sometimes not being sure anyway. I'm an only child, but any family member younger than me at any gathering is always my 'brother' or 'sister'. It can be even more vague. Any person older than me, male or female, can just be referred to as my *pee* and anybody younger is my *nong*. That can sometimes be very confusing for non-Thais, but for us the point is that we are all one big family. On the final day of Songkran, the family was united and together again.

After the special lunch, which had taken hours to prepare, Granny would sit imperiously on a stool while the family members lined up to pay their respects to her, the eldest first. Each knelt on the floor and gently poured a little of the scented water over Granny's cupped hands, while quietly thanking her for her love and guidance throughout the previous year. Granny would flick a little of the water onto the person's head and tie a short piece of sai sin around their wrist, while giving a blessing for good health, good luck and prosperity in the New Year. I was one of the youngest in the family so I would be almost at the end of the line, but that gave me time to work out exactly what I wanted to say to Granny. It couldn't be a casual *Happy New Year, Granny*. I used to think carefully about all her kindness towards me during the previous year, the care she had given me, the things she had taught me and the many little ways I benefitted simply from having her as my granny. It was good to remember those things. I would also kneel before my mother and pour a little of the scented water over her hands, with the same good thoughts. Granny then received small gifts from the adults, usually including a homemade sarong, a blouse, towels and the like, while family members from the city would usually offer small amounts of money. Granny would change into her new clothes and we would then gather round her and spend the rest of the day eating, drinking, laughing and catching up on each other's lives. It was a wonderful day for all of us: a day of unity, harmony and great affection.

Next day, it was back to work for another year.

I feel a little sorry for those Thai youngsters for whom the Songkran Festival is simply an opportunity to run wild on the streets, drenching each other and total strangers with water, and getting drunk for a few days. They're missing out on something very beautiful, very significant—and very Thai.

Saying Goodbye

Granny died in 1991, aged seventy. Her death was followed two years later by that of my mother, who was thirty-nine. Granny had become increasingly unwell over a long period and her death was not unexpected. She knew her time was very close after she claimed she saw the ghosts of her husband and other relatives waiting for her at the bottom of her house steps, a day or so before she died. Although Granny was very superstitious, death didn't frighten her at all. Many of the beliefs and simple everyday rituals that formed a good part of her daily life were animist in origin, but like most Thais she had very realistic and pragmatic Buddhist views about death; views which she had passed on to my mother, as well as to me. Birth, suffering, old age, death: there is no escape for any of us.

At the time Granny died, our little village monastery didn't have a proper crematorium, but that didn't matter to us and we didn't really see much need for one. For centuries in rural areas, corpses were simply taken into a field and burned on a pile of wood, while the mourners stood around and silently watched. That might seem a bit gruesome and undignified to some Westerners, but it was not only the traditional way but also seemed to rural folk the *natural* way to do things. To observe the actual destruction of the corpse by fire was considered a good Buddhist lesson about the impermanent nature of all things. When

I was a child I saw many such cremations, though never one of a close family member till Granny died. By the time of Granny's death, the village monastery had set aside an area in its grounds for cremations, so we didn't have to take corpses to a field. The monastery didn't raise the funds to build a proper crematorium until many years after I left the village.

Although we didn't need a fancy crematorium or great ceremony, there were many simple and traditional Buddhist rites to be performed. They were very important to village folk. It was especially necessary that monks should chant sutras and blessings at the house for several mornings and evenings before the cremation, as well as during and after it. These sutras, about death and the impermanence of all living things, not only comforted the mourners and helped them to accept and understand the death but also, it was believed, helped the deceased on his or her way to a better new life. To further help the dead achieve this better rebirth, it was also very important for family and friends to make merit on the deceased's behalf.

The original cremation area at the monastery was just a small corner of the grounds on which had been built two hefty concrete blocks, about a metre and a half high, three metres long and thirty centimetres thick. The blocks were set parallel to each other, about one and a half metres apart. On the four corners were very tall concrete posts, supporting a metal roof which overhung the crude crematorium. In case of rain, the roof protected the fire and allowed the cremation of the corpse to continue. That was important because it would be very unlucky, as well as unpleasant, if the fire went out before the corpse was completely consumed. The simple lidless wooden coffin was placed on to a metal grid suspended between the two blocks, then oil-soaked wood and other material were piled into the space beneath and the coffin and corpse were burned. The same arrangement is still quite common in remote rural areas even today, if the local monastery doesn't have the funds to build something which, in modern and more sensitive times, might be considered more suitable.

Granny's funeral was a very special occasion for the village and far beyond. She was the village matriarch, herbal doctor and midwife and was well known and greatly respected, not only in our village but in others for kilometres around. Her death was a significant event in the community and hundreds of people wanted to attend the cremation service.

In Thailand, a cremation is usually held up to seven days after the death, though in my village it was nearly always three days. For very important people it can be much longer; as much as a year sometimes, to give plenty of time for merit-making on behalf of the deceased. The delay also gives time for family members working far away to return home to pay their respects to the deceased and offer condolences to the family. During the period between the death and the cremation, Buddhist funeral rites are held every morning and evening, followed by another service seven days after the cremation. My mother and her brothers decided to follow village tradition and hold Granny's cremation three days after she died. Cremations are not usually held on a Friday because the Thai word for Friday is *Wan Suk*, which sounds similar to another Thai word, though spelt differently, meaning 'happiness'.

Granny died peacefully in her house, surrounded by her family and close friends. In some regions the corpse is immediately moved to a monastery but in my village it was the custom to keep it in the house, if that was practical. Granny's body was first washed with jasmine-perfumed water, then dressed in her best clothes. Her hands were placed on her chest in the wai position, with a lotus flower and incense sticks held between them, tied with sai sin string. In many parts of Thailand, the deceased's left arm is placed on the edge of the coffin and mourners gently pour scented water over the hand, but that wasn't a tradition in my village. A small coin was put into Granny's mouth and the corpse was placed in a plain wooden coffin, with the head end pointing towards the West, since that represents the setting or dying sun. The coin was given just in case Granny's spirit needed money to get her started in her next life, though in some regions it serves as a reminder that the dead cannot take their material possessions with them. The coffin was left open and I was quite amazed when I saw Granny's face. She looked beautiful. For the first time in her life—albeit when she was dead—Granny was wearing Western-style make-up.

After Granny was dressed and made-up, the coffin was put inside a large, refrigerated stainless-steel box, borrowed from the monastery. The sealed metal box was placed on two tall wooden tables and draped with brightly coloured flashing fairy lights. To one side was a small table holding a framed photograph of Granny; a very old one, but the only one we had (the one included in this book, in fact). As mourners arrived, each respectfully bowed their head and wai-ed the photograph, then lit a single incense stick and placed it in a sand-filled brass container, on a table in front of the coffin. Three incense sticks are only ever lit together when paying homage to the Buddha. There were very few wreaths from mourners because that wasn't much of a tradition in the village and most people couldn't afford them anyway.

Each morning all the monks came from the village monastery

to the house to chant and to accept breakfast and small gifts from the family mourners. These were offered on Granny's behalf to make merit for her. When all the mourners had arrived, one would knock three times on the head end of the metal box, to let Granny know it was time for breakfast and to listen to the chanting. A tray of breakfast food was placed in front of her photograph. After breakfast the monks chanted blessings, while holding sai sin string which passed through all their hands to Granny's coffin. It was believed the sai sin helped Granny's spirit have contact with the chants and blessings being made on her behalf. Each evening, four monks (traditionally always four) came to the house and, their faces hidden behind ceremonial fans, chanted very long sutras for the dead, which were also symbolically transmitted to Granny's spirit. When the chanting had finished and the monks had returned to the monastery, members of the family and neighbours sat up all night, chatting and playing cards, to keep each other company during the scary time of having a corpse in the house.

As is the custom, early in the morning on the day of the cremation several of my young cousins and I ordained as novice monks, a tradition known as *Buat Na Fai*, 'ordaining in front of the fire'. By ordaining, even just for a day, it is believed that great merit can be transferred to the deceased to help that person move on to a better next life. Unlike the ordination for a monk, novice ordination is a simple ceremony. Each of us, our heads newly shaved, knelt before the abbot and requested that we be ordained. He gave his permission, we changed into our orange robes and then repeated line by line as he recited the ten novice precepts. After the cremation, we disrobed in an equally simple ceremony.

In the early afternoon on the day of the cremation, the coffin was taken out of its refrigerated container to be transported to the monastery. Getting a heavy coffin out of a house and down steep steps in a dignified way can be a problem, but there were many willing hands to help. It's traditional that the dead person should not leave the house by the usual route but it isn't always practical to manhandle a coffin out of a window, so the stairs are sometimes covered in banana leaves or other materials, to make them a little different from usual. For Granny, we carried the coffin down the stairs head end first, instead of the usual way of leaving the house feet first. Once down the stairs, the coffin was loaded on to a large trolley with bicycle wheels, decorated to look like a traditional buffalo cart. The cart was to be pushed to the monastery by several mourners, happy to be of this last service to the revered old lady.

Hundreds of people were waiting at the foot of the stairs to lead the coffin to the monastery. The entire population of the village had turned out, as well as many more people from surrounding communities. Most were wearing black or black and white, though some of the older ladies wore traditional northern Lanna-style ceremonial clothes.

The abbot of the monastery led the procession from the house, followed by other monks and then by the new novices and mourners. All of us were holding sai sin string, which passed through our hands to the coffin. The leading mourner—my mother—carried Granny's photograph and others carried gifts of new robes which were to be offered to the monks on Granny's behalf at the ceremony. Following behind the coffin was a percussion band, playing very mournful funeral music.

Along the way to the monastery, the mourners scattered popped rice grains and flower petals on to the path, from cones made from banana leaves. It was believed that immediately after the cremation the released spirit would be confused and lost, so the trail of rice and petals helped the spirit find its way back home. Seven days after the cremation, there would be a special service held in the house which would finally release the spirit to wherever it was to go, and additionally prevent it staying around as a wandering, lonely ghost.

Because Granny's ancestors originally came from the old Kingdom of Lanna, and she spoke only the Lanna or Khammueang language, the village elders had decided to base part of her cremation ceremony on ancient Lanna traditions. The Lanna Kingdom (*the Kingdom of a Million Rice Fields*) was an independent northern state from the thirteenth to the eighteenth century, before the Thai nation as it is today came into being. In the village there was nobody who knew the Lanna funeral traditions well enough to perform them but an elder from another village came to advise and help out. Some of the traditions are much the same as for an ordinary Thai funeral but with one major exception: the funeral pyre is dramatically set alight using guided rockets.

When the long procession reached the monastery, the cart was first trundled three times in an anti-clockwise direction around the crematorium before the coffin was unloaded and placed on the metal grid between the concrete cremation blocks. The mourners then moved to the *sala*; the chanting and meeting hall. There, the monks sat on a long, high platform and chanted the sutras about impermanence, while the mourners sat listening on the floor. Although there were usually only about ten monks resident at the village monastery, for Granny's funeral seventy had been invited; one for each year of her life. They had come from monasteries from all over the province for this special occasion. I think Granny would have been rather pleased about that.

At the end of the long service in the sala, the mourners moved outside to the cremation area and each was given a small flower fashioned from wood shavings, to which was attached a short length of incense stick and a tiny piece of candle. These were to be made as offerings to Granny but additionally provided easy burning and aromatic fuel for the fire. Outside, family members placed gifts of new robes on the coffin and each was accepted by the most senior monks while they chanted briefly from behind their ceremonial fans. Taking a robe from a corpse is a reminder of the time, more than two thousand years ago, when monks made their own robes from pieces of cloth found on corpses in charnel grounds. The mourners then queued up to tap their offerings of wood flowers and incense three times on the edge of Granny's coffin, before placing them on her body. Each mourner gave a respectful wai and stood for a quiet moment of reflection about Granny's life. Finally, the visiting elder broke a coconut open and gently poured the water over Granny's face and body. Coconut water is considered to be very pure and pouring it on the corpse symbolises purification. The empty coconut shell was then smashed into many pieces on the ground, so that it couldn't be used for any other purpose.

In the coffin, Granny's corpse was face-up and lying on a blanket. For this open type of cremation, the body needs to be face-down. If it's face-up, muscles and sinews can contract and expand in the heat and it's possible for the corpse to seem to stiffly and jerkily sit up in the coffin, or to reach out an arm. Nobody wants to see that happen, so four men give a sharp tug on one side of the blanket, which rolls the corpse onto its front. It may not

I saw that happen in Nepal

sound very dignified, but it's necessary.

Before the procession had arrived, the visiting elder had arranged for the traditional Lanna part of the ceremony. All around the monastery grounds were tall trees. Strings had been tied high up in the trees in the four corners of the monastery. The strings led in a downward trajectory from the trees to the funeral pyre, where they were tied to the posts supporting the roof. Fixed with loops to the strings were large rockets, hidden in the trees. When all was ready, with the mourners standing at a respectable and safe distance, their hands held in a wai, the rockets were fired. With a very noisy *whoosh* and a trail of smoke and flame, the rockets flew down the strings from four directions, passing other fireworks which were hung in the trees and which exploded with loud bangs or in a shower of colourful sparks. The rockets simultaneously hit the coffin and oil-soaked wood, which with a load roar immediately burst into flames. It was very noisy, dramatic and quite spectacular.

I know Granny would have been very proud and happy with her sendoff.

Once everything was ablaze, the funeral director who had special knowledge about such things had to occasionally turn the corpse with a green bamboo pole, to make sure that it burned evenly. The cremation itself took about two hours but all the mourners stayed to silently watch. Most of them, I think, were contemplating death and the impermanent nature of life. I was thinking about the wonderful years I had spent with Granny, of the love and care she had given me, of all the fun we'd had together and the many wonderful things she had taught me. But I was only eleven years old and although I had seen open cremations before, I had never been so close to one as a member of the family. I was very distressed when Granny's body had to be turned by the funeral director, but as a novice monk I couldn't show any emotion. I was determined not to cry anyway because when my friend Supot died a few years before, Granny told me that if I cried at his funeral his spirit would drown in my tears.

The fire was left smoldering all night, reducing everything but the largest bones to ashes. Next day, my uncle and I buried Granny's smaller remains in a small chedi-shaped tin urn under a pho tree in the monastery grounds, where her own parents' remains were buried. The larger bones were buried respectfully but without ceremony in a pit. Because of the Thai people's pragmatic attitude towards death, our funerals are not usually the tearful events they can be in Western countries and we don't have or need long mourning periods afterwards. Following Granny's cremation, everybody went straight back to work and life just carried on as usual.

My mother also had to leave the village very soon after the cremation to return to her building job in Samut Sakhon. With Granny gone, there was nobody to take fulltime care of me. I know Mother didn't want to leave me on my own but she had to earn money to support both of us, which she couldn't do in the village. She was still determined that I would start my studies at high school, so she needed to save money to cover those expenses. I understood that she had to go. That was a lonely and difficult time for me, though I had an aunt and uncle living nearby who gave me considerable support.

My mother was generous, kind-hearted and very popular in the village. She had many friends there, though she was not as well known as Granny beyond our limited borders. In her daily life she wasn't as superstitious as her own mother, I suppose because she was one generation removed—more modern—just as I am from her. Despite not being particularly superstitious, mother still followed many of the old ways and it was she who wanted Granny's funeral to be as traditional as possible, to please the old lady. Mother would have wanted the same traditional type of funeral for herself, but maybe without the pyrotechnics.

The farming life wasn't easy in Granny's or Mother's time. Farmers struggled along, resignedly accepting their situation, but with the consolation that they would depart this life with family and friends making merit on their behalf, to help them towards what they hoped would be a better rebirth. Nobody looked forward to death but at least they had the comfort of knowing they would have a proper funeral. Sadly, for my mother, that wasn't to be.

Even now, many years later, I still feel great unhappiness about my mother's death and her makeshift cremation. I can pragmatically accept her actual death, but I am still so sorry that we weren't able to give her the traditional funeral rites and merit-making that she deserved and would have wanted.

About eighteen months after Granny's death, I received a letter from my mother's friend in Samut Sakhon to say that my mother was very ill. I immediately wanted to go to see her, but it was a long way to travel alone for a child and I had only a few baht. My relatives in the village didn't have any money either, but they assured me that it probably wasn't necessary to go and that my mother would be fine. I didn't go. Soon after, I had another letter from the friend to say that my mother was dead. My uncles immediately borrowed money from wealthier neighbours so we could make the long journey by bus and train to collect her body and bring it back to the village. We wanted to give Mother a traditional village funeral surrounded by her family, neighbours and friends, with lots of merit-making, exactly as she would have wanted.

Unfortunately, after we collected the body in Samut Sakhon, the railway authority refused to let us transport the simple wooden coffin back to our province unless we had all the necessary and complicated official forms, as well as an approved outer coffin. My uncles were confused about what to do. They didn't have enough money to buy the outer coffin, nor to rent a van to take the original coffin back to the village, so they sadly and reluctantly decided to hold the cremation in a monastery in Samut Sakhon. None of us liked the idea; the abbot and monks there didn't know my mother or us, or our village traditions, so it all seemed so impersonal. Granny would have said it wasn't the *right* way to do things. My uncles also hadn't come prepared with enough money for a proper three-day funeral, with everything that entailed, but they had little choice and tried to do the best they could in the circumstances. Basically, we were faced with disposing of a corpse that was already several days old, so it had to be done quickly. There wasn't even time for me to ordain as a novice for the day.

The body was cremated in a ten-minute ceremony on the steps of the crematorium, with just four monks to briefly chant. Very late that same night, we returned to our own province by bus and train, with me holding my mother's still warm remains in my lap, in a small cardboard box. When we got back, my uncle helped me bury them under the tree in the village monastery, next to the ashes of my granny. To this day, whenever I visit the village, my uncle apologises to me for the sad way he had to handle my mother's funeral.

Some weeks after my mother's death, I ordained again as a

novice at the village monastery but almost immediately moved to a big city monastery far away, to start my high school studies at the free monastic school. I somehow knew, even as I left the village, that I would never permanently return. I had just turned thirteen. And so ended my days as a village boy.

I still miss my mother and Granny very much.

Explanatory Notes
and More Folk Tales

*Note 1, page 22: **What your mole says about you***

Despite her many superstitions, Granny didn't seem to place much credibility on being able to tell someone's character or future from marks on their body. She said that farmers didn't need to be told their futures because they already knew what they would be: working till they dropped dead. But many Thai people, especially city folk, do seem to find the marks and their meanings fascinating and credible. There are dozens of moles and birthmarks on various parts of the body that are believed to indicate a person's character and future and their meanings are often lengthy and very precise. These, briefly, are the main characteristics of some of the moles or birthmarks on the face:

On the upper forehead: This man has what Thais call *chaidi*—a good heart. He is confident and prepared to work hard to achieve his personal goals. He has artistic ideas and likes to have a hobby. For a woman, the mark indicates a strong sense of morality and justice but she may also be insecure and jealous of others. She is likely to marry a man who has been married before and he will probably be more intelligent than she is.

On the middle forehead: This man is intelligent, fun-loving and high-spirited. He enjoys his freedom and prefers an older partner, though he may have difficulty establishing a lasting relationship with one. A woman with a mark in this position should look out for a man with a similar mark because they could be well-suited. She will probably not meet her ideal partner until she is past her youth but meanwhile she will have plenty of opportunities for romance.

Over the left or right temple: This man may have some problems in his teens, especially about love and money. He will have a better time in his early twenties, by which time he will be well-respected by others for his charm and strong sense of morality. He shouldn't consider getting married until he is in his late twenties and should look for a partner younger than himself. A woman with the same mark may also have had a difficult time in her youth, though hers may have been caused by health problems. Her future in middle life could be good and she may marry a very wealthy man. Even if she doesn't marry well, she is likely to receive a large amount of money from some unexpected source.

Between the eyebrows: Despite having had a difficult childhood, this man will be lucky in later life. He is a generally good person, intelligent and with excellent business sense. Although usually lucky, he may have difficulty finding a suitable partner but when he does, the relationship will be a strong one. For a woman, the mark indicates charm, sensitivity and intelligence. She is careful in everything she does and will be successful in her employment. Although she will never be poor, she shouldn't marry a man with more money than she has—the relationship won't work out very well.

On the left or right eyebrow: This man wants everything

that life has to offer and is quite likely to achieve it. He enjoys spending money and showing off his wealth but money won't necessarily bring him great happiness. He is likely to be unlucky in love and may have several difficult relationships before settling on a final partner. Although a woman with a mark on her eyebrow may be financially successful, she could have difficulty hanging on to her wealth, especially as she gets older. She enjoys social activities, especially those associated with art and music. Her best relationship will be with an older partner who might be a foreigner.

On the left cheek: This man has a strong sex drive and appetite. He will have many partners but his most successful relationship will be with a woman who has already been married several times. He is well-liked, especially by people of his own age, because of his politeness and neat personal presentation. A woman with a mark on the left cheek also has a strong sex drive but she enjoys playing games with her partner, sometimes seeking to make him jealous. She is ambitious and fun-loving and enjoys travel and meeting many new people.

On the right cheek: Oh dear, this is one mole that some Thai fortune tellers recommend should be removed. Although this man may have some good qualities, he is likely to be over-emotional and can cause hurt to others because he doesn't stop to think about his words or actions. He may also be quite selfish. That may be due to his upbringing, when he was an unhappy and unpleasant child. He's usually not very clever and will have to make a great effort if he is to achieve anything positive in life. A women with this mark is likely to be lazy, dull and somewhat stupid. She enjoys sex and the power she thinks this gives her over her partner. Although she doesn't have a very positive character, she may achieve a shallow sort of happiness, especially as she may marry a wealthy man.

Note 2, page 27: Granny's wedding

In rural areas in Granny's time there was no wedding ceremony in the form it is usually known, with vows and rings exchanged before a priest and with legal documents to be signed. In my village, the engagement was as significant as the wedding and both ceremonies were usually held on the same day. The ceremony was always followed or preceded by a blessing from monks at the local monastery. The head monk would explain the duties of a man to his future wife and vice versa, but monks are not priests and there is no Buddhist marriage service. Marriages might later be legally formalised by registering the union at the local city hall, but in Granny's time that was rarely done by village folk. City hall was far away and difficult to get to, and it wasn't considered necessary to register the marriage anyway.

On the morning of her wedding, Granny would have waited in her parent's house for the groom to arrive. Both bride and groom would be wearing their best traditional Lanna-style clothes. Neither would have bought a special gown or suit, though Granny may have made herself a new sarong and blouse on her cotton loom. The groom would have approached the house carrying the agreed dowry gifts, as well as gifts for the bride's parents. The bride's gifts traditionally included young banana trees and sugar cane plants, which would eventually provide nourishment for any babies that were born to the couple. Following the groom would be a rowdy and probably drunken procession of his family, friends and supporters, accompanied by a loud percussion band.

As the procession neared the house, the path would be barred by a 'gate'—the silver gate. The silver gate was traditionally a length of silver chain stretched across the path but in poor rural communities it might be no more than a piece of string suspended between two cut banana stems, forming an arch. The gate was guarded by the bride's relatives. Before the procession could pass through, the guards would ask what the groom wanted. He would reply that he wanted to get married. There would be lots of teasing from both sides, but the guards wouldn't let the groom pass until he had proved he could financially support his bride-to-be by paying a silver toll—the key to the gate. The toll might be a silver coin or some trinket with a silvery sheen. The guards would jokingly protest that the payment wasn't enough and demand more, or insist on gifts for themselves as well, but eventually they would let the groom pass, accompanied by great cheering from his supporters.

Soon after, the procession would arrive at a second gate—the gold gate. Again, the guards would demand toll money as a key to the gate, but that time in gold. A few low-value golden satang coins would change hands, and the procession could continue to the house.

On arrival at the house, the bride would show her respect and allegiance to her husband-to-be by washing his feet. Granny did so, but in modern and more gender-equal times it is rarely done, even in rural areas. The groom would then present the dowry gifts to the bride's parents for their inspection and approval. There might have been some friendly banter about the poor value of the gifts, but they would finally be accepted. Waist-length garlands of jasmine flowers would then be hung around the necks of the bride and groom.

A village elder presided over the marriage ceremony. The bride and groom would kneel before him, with the groom on the right. The elder would place two joined loops of specially prepared thick sai sin cotton around the heads of both bride and groom. The circles of sai sin, known in this ceremony as s*ai mongkhon,* symbolise the linking together of the couple, as well as continuity in the union. The elder would then pour consecrated perfumed water over the joined hands of the couple, which rested on large silver bowls containing many different kinds of flowers and petals. The foreheads of the new couple would be anointed by the elder with white chalk paste. Family members and guests would also bless the newlyweds by pouring water over their hands and then by tying sai sin around the couple's wrists. During the ceremony, guests would usually present the new couple with small amounts of money and other gifts.

In the evening, the house and its surrounding area would be packed with villagers eating, drinking, dancing and generally having a good time. Much rice whisky would be consumed. At the end of the festivities, the newlyweds would be escorted to their marriage 'bed': usually just a pile of blankets laid on a bamboo floor mat. Since the house was just one big room, an area would have been temporarily partitioned off for their use. Inside, the room would have been decorated with fertility symbols, good luck charms and bags of rice, and an elderly married couple would be found sitting on the bed. Before they left the room, the elderly couple would tell the newlyweds how comfortable the bed was and how lucky it felt, subtly hinting that the newlyweds would have many children.

After they were married, the newlyweds would continue living

In china the bride goes to the husband's family home!!

at the bride's family home, until their own new house was built.

Note 3, page 30: The village shop

The first shop opened in the village in about 1989, though it wasn't really a shop in the usual sense. It was just a small area in front of someone's house with a few tables for displaying goods, but it was still an exciting event. The shop sold a small and random collection of everyday things which we had difficulty getting; fuel oil for kerosene lamps, light bulbs, hardware, plastic combs, mirrors, a few cosmetics and so on. Because getting to the city involved such a long and difficult journey, we usually had to rely on visiting sellers for such things if we needed them.

Amongst the shop's limited opening stock were a few tins and packets of food. I had never seen tinned food before and I was fascinated, especially by the idea of fish in a tin can, like sardines. I desperately wanted to try some. '*What on earth for?*' asked Granny. She reminded me that we were surrounded by food, including fish, and that we were never hungry. If we wanted something to eat we could go out and catch it or pick it—free. She was quite right. My family never needed to spend a single baht to buy food but to me the idea of fish in a tin can was still irresistible. I had to wait several more years, until I was a novice monk in a city monastery and walked on my daily alms round, before anybody put a tin of sardines in my alms bowl. Even then, the tin was without a ring-pull and I hadn't a clue how to open it, never having seen a tin opener in my life. I spent a long time banging at the top of the tin with a knife before the mutilated container finally split open.

I was reminded of that years later on one of my return visits to the village. The original shop was still there but by then was considerably larger and with a much wider range of goods, most of them plastic, and with many more prepackaged food items. What surprised me was that the village women seemed to be queuing up to buy the goods, as though the fields and forest surrounding them had suddenly run out of free, fresh food.

Note 4, page 39: Telling time Thai style

Traditionally, Thais split the day into four periods of six hours each and start counting from 6: 6 am Western time is also 6 Thai time, but 7 am becomes 1, 8 am becomes 2, 9 am becomes 3, 10 am becomes 4, 11 am becomes 5 and 12 midday is noon. Similarly in the evening quarter, 6 pm is 6 but 7 pm becomes 1, 8 pm becomes 2 and so on. Additional words are added before or after the number to indicate which of the four periods is being referred to. For example, 10 am in Thai would be *sip mong chao: sip* being Thai for 'ten' and *mong chao* referring to the late morning period. There is logic in this but even now, years later, when I look at a clock on which the hand is clearly pointing to the ten, I will still say in English '*four in the morning*', often causing great confusion if I am talking to a non-Thai.

Note 5, page 39: Thai monks do not beg

Some visitors to Thailand assume that when monks walk on their daily alms round they are begging for food and that their alms bowls are begging bowls. Monks do not beg and are not allowed to ask for anything from laypeople. In his book *Phra Farang* (written when he was a monk), co-author Peter Robinson described his city alms round in this way:

'The ceremony of offering food is simple but full of symbolism. The layperson waits at the side of the road with a basket or tray of food, usually rice and curries packed in little plastic bags, a piece of fruit and perhaps a cake or other sweet. The monk approaches with eyes downcast, looking only at the pavement, mindful of every step. As the monk draws near, the layperson invites him to accept food by saying "*nimmon*". Without looking up, the monk stops walking and stands perfectly still. These few moments of complete stillness enable the donor to consider the merit of his or her action and the monk to contemplate the meaning of the food as a support and necessity for his body. Then, bending forward very slightly from the waist, the monk raises the lid of his bowl and the donor gently places the food inside. The monk should not look at the donor, but keeps his full attention on the bowl. The donor pays respect to the monk with a graceful wai, the lid of the bowl is lowered, and the monk walks on his way. The monk should never say "*thank you*", but occasionally may murmur a short blessing in Pali. Usually, no words are spoken and none are necessary. Both monk and layperson are aware that they have followed a tradition that has barely changed for thousands of years'

Note 6, page 68: Granny's herbal remedies

There are hundreds of herbs, plants and roots used in traditional

Thai medicine. The following are some I remember Granny using on a regular basis, often to treat my own childhood ailments, and others that I have heard about and which are still used by healers in rural communities. Although each of these herbs has its own medicinal properties, Granny didn't always use them individually in her remedies. Sometimes she would use several different ingredients in different forms, and always in very precise quantities. I can't give any instructions for preparing these remedies because unfortunately Granny never left a recipe book.

Although few traditional herbal remedies have side-effects, there are some herbs which are poisonous if not prepared properly and used in precise amounts. In modern times, herbs and other plants collected in the wild may contain chemical pesticides or be contaminated on their surfaces. A few poisonous plants also look very similar to harmless ones, so great caution is needed before using them. There are many excellent and very professional printed guides to the properties and use of traditional Thai herbal medicines, so please refer to them or a herbal expert before using any of the following:

Camphor (*Cinnamonum camphora*): Camphor crystals were frequently used by Granny in her hot compresses after a hard day in the paddy fields. When working in the fields, farmers were often bitten by insects or suffered minor cuts and abrasions, and camphor was a good cure. Granny also used camphor in her postnatal treatments.

Cassumunar Ginger (*Zingiber cassumunar*): I don't recall Granny ever using this herb for me, but she often used it to help ease her own aching muscles and joints after an exhausting day in the paddy fields. She would mash it up and add a couple of other ingredients, then mix it with water and spread it over the aching areas. She also used it in her hot herbal compresses.

Chirata (*Carthamus tinctorius*): Tea made from the leaves of chirata was one of Granny's remedies for colds, flu, sore throat and bronchitis. She gave it to me several times and I always dreaded it because it is very bitter and always made me feel a little sick. It worked, though. Granny also recommended chewing the stalks of the plant for toothache.

Culantro (*Eryngium foetidum*): Besides using this plant in her cooking, Granny recommended it as a tea drink for use as a laxative. She would also grind it into a paste with a little water that had previously been used to cook rice and use it as an ointment for venomous insect bites.

Galangal (*Alpinia galanga*): Granny often used galangal to treat my insect bites as a child. Chopped up and boiled, the water was also used to treat nausea, stomachache and diarrhoea.

Garlic (*Allium sativum*): Although garlic has many uses in traditional Thai medicine, Granny seemed to use it most often to stop my childhood nose bleeds. She would take the skin of the garlic and chop it up with dried mulberry leaves and camphor, wrap them in a dried banana leaf like a cheroot and let me take a few puffs, blowing the smoke out through my nose. The nose bleed would stop almost immediately. I also remember one time when I had an ear infection and Granny put a few drops of garlic juice in my ear.

Kaffir lime (*Citrus hystix*): Whenever I had a cold or cough, Granny would make a hot infusion of kaffir lime for me to inhale, with my head under a blanket. Taken internally, it was good for indigestion. Granny also used the leaves and fruit in her herbal sauna postnatal treatments. Granny never used modern chemical shampoo and instead would bake several limes on a fire until the skins were brown, then cut them in half and rub them over her hair before rinsing off. Left whole around a bed, the limes also deter snakes and centipedes, because they apparently don't like the smell.

Kasot/Cassod (*Cassia simea*): Granny used kasot quite frequently for villagers who couldn't sleep or were stressed or nervous. She would make a decoction from several parts of the tree, including the wood, shoots and leaves, and leave it for several days in alcohol before using it. I believe Granny Perng, the village Ghost Doctor, also used kasot sometimes, probably for the calming effect it produced in her neurotic or 'possessed' patients.

Lemongrass (*Cymbopogon citratus*): Besides being an ingredient in much of Granny's cooking, she used lemongrass for many minor ailments, including colds, fever, sore throat, flatulence and indigestion. She also regularly made a hot tea drink with lemongrass, specifically to help ease her own back and joint pains.

Monkey Jack (*Artocarpus lakoocha*): I recall one summer in the village when several children suffered from intestinal worms, though I didn't, thankfully. The preparation of Granny's remedy was quite complicated and involved boiling small pieces of monkey jack wood in a pan and collecting the thick scum from the surface. When the scum dried, it became an orangey-yellow powder, which Granny then ground very fine. The powder was mixed with a little water and drunk.

Nat leaf (*Blumea balsamifera*): Nat leaf was used by Granny for many different purposes, alone or in combination with other ingredients. For her postnatal treatments, nat leaf would be boiled in water, which would then be used for washing the new mother's body. The liquid was also drunk. As a body wash, I remember it was particularly effective for curing itchy skin, particularly after I had a swim in the village canal. Nat leaf water could also be drunk to cure headache, nausea, gall stones and to help with low blood pressure. Mashed up, the leaf makes a good ointment for skin ailments like boils, scratches and minor wounds. The leaf can also be smoked in a cheroot to help sinus problems. Nat is now much utilised in TTM aromatherapy treatments.

Nim/Neem (*Azadirachta indica*): Granny used every part of the nim tree in her various preparations and remedies, including the stem bark, root bark, heartwood, shoots, leaves, seeds and fruit. Various parts of the tree could be used as a general tonic, and for nausea, fever, haemorrhoids, malaria, indigestion, food poisoning, dysentery, diarrhoea, vomiting and for internal parasites. Nim oil was used for mouth ulcers and other oral infections. Nim was also used by Granny as an insecticide in the paddy fields.

Oroxylum (*Oroxylum indicum*): This was one of the ingredients in Granny's Bone Blower treatments, applied as a poultice to small broken bones. She also used it as an ointment for minor burns, cuts and wounds.

Safflower (*Carthamus tinctorius*): Granny always kept a small store of dried safflower flowers at the ready because she had a few patients with menstruation problems. She would usually prescribe hot tea made from the flowers, to be drunk several times a day. Granny also recommended eating sesame seeds for the same problem, though they needed no preparation.

Turmeric (*Curcuma longa*): Turmeric is a member of the ginger family and was used by Granny mashed up as a general antiseptic and antibacterial agent for cuts, burns and bruises. Granny often prescribed it to village lads to clear up their adolescent spots and acne, when it would be mixed with chalk powder and spread on the face. It can be taken internally for indigestion, flatulence and other gastrointestinal discomfort. Granny also used it in her herbal compresses for massaging her own aching neck muscles. I never saw Granny use turmeric for a cobra bite but I have heard that it can help in emergencies, until anti-venom is administered. Turmeric also protects the skin from mosquitoes and ants.

Wan Chak Motluk (*Curcuma comosa*): Granny used this sedge bulb as a key ingredient in her Yu Fai postnatal treatment. It helps heal the womb.

Note 7 , page 78: How long was the python?

In Granny's day, rural people didn't use metres or feet as units of measurement. They used a *wah* which was the length of the stretched-out arms from fingertip to fingertip. That meant, of course, that my one wah (me having short arms) might be less than your one wah, but for any individual wanting to describe the length or width of something *in relation to themselves*, it was still a reasonably accurate measurement. The wah is still used as a measurement in Thailand but is now taken to be precisely equivalent to two metres.

Note 8, page 110: Mae Nak: the most feared and famous ghost of all.

There's no historical evidence that this story is true but it first appeared in the mid-1800s, when a newlywed couple, Tid and

Nang Nak, moved into an abandoned house in Bangkok's Phra Kanong District. (Nang, the wife, later became known as Mae—*mother*—Nak).

Tid Nak, the husband, was a soldier and had to leave home to fight in a war soon after the couple was married. Nang begged him not to go or leave her alone, but Tid had no choice. Nang was already pregnant then with the couple's first child, but she and the baby died during childbirth while Tid was away. Nang had loved and pined for her husband so much that she and the baby became ghosts and remained in human form, waiting for Tid to return from his military duty. Tid didn't know his wife and child were dead. When he eventually returned home, neighbours told him of their deaths but Tid refused to believe them, since he could clearly see his wife and child. He didn't realise that Nang had placed a spell on him and he continued to live with her in the old house. Neighbours who tried to warn him of his danger later died in horrible circumstances.

One evening, Tid was watching his wife prepare dinner. She accidentally dropped a lime through the floor boards of the house and onto the earth below. Tid saw Nang extend her arm by two metres as she reached to retrieve the lime. Horrified, he realised that the neighbours had told him the truth and he ran terrified from the house. Nang chased after him, begging him to return, but Tid took refuge inside a nearby temple, which as a ghost Nang couldn't enter. She was so angry that she began to terrorise the local people of Phra Kanong, causing havoc and many violent deaths.

Nang's ghost was eventually captured by a powerful exorcist and imprisoned within an earthenware jar, which was wrapped in cloth on which was written a powerful spell to prevent Nang's ghost escaping. The jar was thrown into the river but was later found by fishermen who couldn't read the spell and didn't know what the jar contained. They opened it and Nang's angry ghost escaped. She again caused many violent deaths in the Phra Kanong district before she was recaptured. That time, the ghost was restrained by a famous and powerful monk. In one version of the story he confined the ghost within a piece of the skull of Nang's own corpse and bound the bone inside his waistband. In another version, the monk told Nang that if she left Tid and the locals in peace, she would eventually be reunited with her husband in a future life. Either way, the ghost was finally subdued.

Local people later began to feel pity for Nang Nak, so they erected a shrine to her in the monastery and invited her spirit and her baby's spirit to stay there. Now known as Mae (mother) Nak, the shrine draws thousands of visitors every year, who lay gold leaf on the statue of Mae Nak and her baby and leave gifts of food, clothing and toys. A television is left running facing the shrine, because apparently Mae Nak quite enjoys Thai soap operas.

Note 9, page 124: The Royal Ploughing Ceremony

We didn't have television or newspapers in the village so I don't think Granny had heard of the Royal Ploughing Ceremony, but if she had she would certainly have approved since it combines rice, tradition and His Majesty The King.

Two beautiful oxen lower their huge heads to eat from a selection of food laid out on banana leaf platters in front of them. They are watched closely by members of the Thai Royal family, Brahmin priests and thousands of rural farmers, because the oxen's choice of food could predict whether the coming growing season will be bountiful or not. The seven different foods—rice, corn, green beans, sesame, grass, water and whisky—signify different things, both alone and in combination. If the oxen choose to eat rice or corn, there will be a good harvest of grains and fruit. If they eat sesame, hay and drink water, there will be plenty of rain. Drinking the alcohol will mean a healthy economy and successful foreign trade.

This is the Royal Ploughing Ceremony, an ancient Brahmin ritual held at the beginning of the rice-growing season. The ceremony is held in May on a date decided by a court astrologer and has been held since the time of the Sukhothai Kingdom (1238–1438). It was discontinued in 1936 but revived in 1960 by the present monarch, King Bhumibol Adulyadej. His Majesty The King or his representative always attends the ceremony. The ceremony was originally purely Brahmin but Buddhist elements were added during the reign of King Mongkut (1804–1868).

The ceremony lasts two days and has two parts. In each, a senior official from the Ministry of Agriculture assumes the role of Lord of the Harvest (*Phraya Raek Na*), assisted by four Celestial Maidens (*Thephi*): senior unmarried women officials from the Ministry.

On the first day is the Cultivating Ceremony, a mixed Buddhist and Brahmin ritual, held in the Royal Chapel of the Temple of the Emerald Buddha and presided over by His Majesty The King or his representative. Blessings are sought from Brahmin deities on forty kilograms of rice and forty varieties of crop seeds, including glutinous rice, sorghum, sesame seeds, taro, potato, gourd seeds, melon and sweet basil. The grains come from the experimental farm in the grounds of His Majesty's palace and will be used in the next day's ceremony. The Lord of the Harvest and the Celestial Maidens receive a blessing from the King who then presents the Lord of the Harvest with ceremonial items to be used in the Ploughing Ceremony. Homage with candles and incense is also paid to the Buddha.

The Ploughing Ceremony itself is held on the second day on Sanam Luang (the Royal Ground) in front of the Temple of the Emerald Buddha. It begins with the Lord of the Harvest predicting the amount of rain which will fall in the coming growing season, which he does by choosing one of three pieces of cloth of different lengths. The shortest piece predicts a year with too much rain, the longest warns of possible shortage of water and the medium-sized cloth indicates a balanced rainfall, abundant rice and healthy crops.

With the two oxen, the Lord of the Harvest then ploughs the ground, using a wooden plough decorated in red and gold. Three furrows are ploughed and the Lord of the Harvest scatters the forty different types of rice grains from gold and silver trays carried by the Celestial Maidens, while Brahmin priests dressed in robes of white and gold chant and blow through conch shells. After the ploughing, the oxen are released to make their all important choice of food.

When the ceremony is over, hundreds of rice farmers from all over the country who have come to witness the ceremony surge onto the Sanam Luang ground to look for grains of rice. They keep them for good luck or mix them with their own rice stock, to ensure a good harvest.

Note 10, page 143: The legend of the Mlabri

The Mlabri are the most primitive and least known of Thailand's ethnic groups. They live in the far northern provinces of Nan and Phrae. Like Granny's mysterious pygmies, the Mlabri also build temporary shelters from banana leaves and move on when the leaves turn yellow, but they are not pygmies and their feet are a normal shape. Because until recently they were so rarely seen outside their jungle or forest environment, they were known to Thais as *Phi Tong Luang*—Spirits of the Yellow Leaves.

The Mlabri were unknown outside of Thailand until they were 'discovered' in the deep jungle by Europeans in the late 1930s. Partly because they were hunter-gatherers and had not developed agricultural skills, anthropologists thought at first that the Mlabri were a lingering Stone Age remnant which had somehow remained hidden for thousands of years in the jungle. Recent research is casting doubts on that theory.

There is a strange story about the founding of the Mlabri. The Tin Prai, another ethnic people living in the same region, have a legend that centuries ago two of their children were banished and set adrift on a river raft. The Tin Prai had farming skills but the banished children—a boy and a girl—survived in the mountainous jungle by hunting and foraging. They eventually formed their own nomadic tribe, the Mlabri—People of the Forest. They were very secretive and quickly moved to a new location if they felt their presence had been discovered by outsiders. The tribe wore only loincloths made from leaves and bark.

Recent scientific and linguistic research seem to partly support the Tin Prai's legend of the founding of the Mlabri. Tests apparently indicate that the entire known Mlabri population are almost genetically identical and could be descended from just one female and between one and four males, who lived between 500–1,000 years ago. The language of the Mlabri also supports the legend since some researchers claim it is linguistically related to that of the Tin Prai. Until they were 'discovered' and were persuaded to leave the forest, the Mlabri were reported to be childlike in their thinking, possibly because of the young age of their original ancestors.

The Mlabri's own custom forbids the owning of land, so those who have left the jungle now work as labourers on farms, though an American missionary group is helping them to become established in making and exporting hammocks. There are now probably only between 200–300 Mlabri remaining.

Note 11, page 148: The Erawan Shrine

The most well known spirit shrine in Thailand is outside the Grand Hyatt Erawan Hotel in Bangkok. The original shrine was erected in 1956 after a number of accidents and injuries to workers on the site, soon after construction of the hotel started. Other misfortunes plagued the building, including the loss at sea of a ship bringing marble for use in the construction. It was discovered that the foundation stone of the building had been laid on an inauspicious date. Superstitious labourers refused to work on the site, so the hotel owners were advised to quickly erect a spirit shrine. The original name of the hotel was simply 'Erawan', which is the name of the three-headed elephant ridden by Brahma, Lord of the Heavens, so it was decided that the shrine should be dedicated to him. The shrine was built and the accidents stopped.

The Erawan shrine is visited by thousands of people every year who leave gifts, particularly of wooden horses and elephants. Supplicants ask for various favours and, if granted, they will return with more gifts.

The shrine is considered of such great spiritual significance by Thais that when a man seriously vandalised it with a hammer in 2006, he was killed by enraged onlookers. The damaged shrine was quickly replaced, using as much of the original material as possible.

Note 12, page 152: The auspicious trees—and some which are not so lucky

There are nine trees which are considered auspicious to have growing in the family compound or close to the house. Some of the trees grow to thirty or forty metres tall, so although they were suitable for the large compounds or gardens of people of nobility and rank, they couldn't be grown in the more limited area that most ordinary people, like Granny, had available. She planted only a few of the smaller trees. Traditionally, the trees should be planted in a specific order and in specific places in the compound. The first eight trees on this list were planted in order clockwise around the compound, with the ninth—the Jackfruit—in the centre.

The Pink Cassia or Javanese Cassia (*Cassia javanica Linn*) grows to a height of about fifteen metres and bears pink flowers. Being so stately, the tree helps ensure that the owner's high rank is maintained.

The Laburnum (*Cassia fistula Linn*) reaches a height of

between ten and twenty metres and blossoms in cascades of brilliant yellow flowers. The tree is also known as the Golden Shower Tree or Pudding Piper Tree. Grown in the compound, the tree helps the owner gain power and respect. The Laburnum is Thailand's national tree and in the past its wood was used to make flagpoles, plough handles and cart wheels. In Ayurvedic medicine the tree is known as Aragvadha (*disease killer*) and all parts of the tree, except the poisonous seeds, were much used by Granny for treatment of constipation, fever, colds, flu and skin infections, arthritis and hemorrhage.

The Coral (*Erythrina orientalis Linn*) ensures wealth and material success for the compound owner. The tree grows up to about fifteen metres and has claw-shaped orangey-red blossoms.

Bamboo (*Genus phyllostachys*) is actually a type of grass, rather than a tree, but it is considered auspicious because it ensures that the owner's ambitions will be fulfilled and that he will make good progress in life.

The Tembusa (*Wrightia arborea*) gives the owner protection against all types of danger. Granny used the leaves of the tree to treat malaria and asthma.

The Kalamona (*Senna cassia*) is a tall shrub of up to about seven metres with clusters of bright yellow flowers. It is the seed pods that are considered auspicious because they help the owner reach his personal goals. The Kalamona is also known as the Scrambled Egg Tree.

The Teak (*Tectona grandis*) grows to a height of thirty metres or more and is associated with strength, stability, success and power. A major tourist site in Bangkok is the Giant Swing, made from teak, which was erected in 1784 by King Rama I, originally for use in Brahmin New Year ceremonies. The swing was renovated in 1920 and 1959 but in 2003 it was discovered that the pillars had deteriorated and needed to be replaced. Six Teak trees, each about twenty-five metres tall and fifty centimetres in diametre, were cut from northern forests and used to construct the new Giant Swing, which was opened by His Majesty The King in 2007. One of the new trees was scientifically calculated to be ninety-nine years old (a very auspicious number in Thailand) and is being used to clone one million more trees, which will be presented to His Majesty The King for distribution to the people.

The Thailand Rosewood (*Dalbergia cochinchinensis*) protects its owner from enemies, gives him mental strength and reinforces a sense of personal prestige. The tree grows to about twenty metres tall and bears a large purple flower.

The Jackfruit (*Artocarpus heterophyllus)* grows to about fifteen metres tall and produces an enormous and very heavy fruit; the largest tree fruit in the world. The skin of the fruit can be used in cooking, while the bright yellow flesh segments are one of the most popular Thai fruits. The wood of the tree is often used to make musical instruments and furniture.

There are also trees which are considered unlucky to have growing near the family house. Surprisingly, amongst them is one of the most beautiful—the Frangipani (*Plumeria*). With its large, creamy-coloured or pinkish blossoms the tree is very decorative but its name in Thai—*lanthom*—is similar in sound to the word *rathom*, which means 'sorrow'. Some Thai people believe unhappy spirits live in the tree.

Crown flower (*Calotropis gigantea*) grows to four metres tall and has a split personality. It's unlucky because in former times its white flowers were made into garlands and hung around the necks of prisoners due for execution. The flowers are also traditionally used as decoration at funerals. On the other hand, its name in Thai is *Rak* which means 'love', so in modern times the flowers may be used as garlands for a bride and groom to wear at their wedding.

Canna lily (*Cannaceae*) is not usually grown inside the family compound but is often seen making a border or fence around the property. The large, beautiful yellow or red flowers are believed to deter spirits. In Thailand, the plant is known as *Phuttharaksa*.

Asoka *(Saraka indica)* is also known as Ashoka and originally comes from India, where its name in Sanskrit means 'without sorrow'—quite a lucky name. However, in Thai the first syllable of the word is not pronounced, changing the meaning to 'sorrow' and therefore making the tree unlucky to have in the compound. The tree bears a red fruit which is extremely bitter and not usually eaten. In Buddhist legends, the Buddha's mother—Queen Maya—gave birth to her son under an Asoka tree.

Kluai Tani is a banana tree which can be the home of a sometimes malicious and sexually insatiable female spirit called *Nang Tani*. It's not a good idea to have her tree in the family compound.

Although the wood of the Takhian tree (*Hopea odorata* is used for making boats, it isn't used in house building and the tree is not welcome in the compound. The tree grows to a height of about thirty metres and is home to a spirit named *Nang Takhian*, who entices young men to her by singing a mournful song. When the victim approaches the tree, Nang Takhian squeezes the life out of him.

Note 13, page 164: Elephantiasis

Elephants do not, of course, cause elephantiasis. The disease is usually caused by various microscopic parasitic worms which live in the human lymphatic system and which are transmitted by mosquitoes. The disease, or the lymphatic response to it, causes swelling in the lower torso, male genitals and female breasts. Elephantiasis may also be caused by frequent contact with soil or clay which contain high levels of potassium and sodium.

Note 14, page 174: Takraw

When I was a youngster in the village, all the boys played takraw regularly. It was probably more popular than football then, since at that time we didn't have much access to television and weren't able to watch international football games. Takraw is Thailand's national sport and is traditionally played by two competing teams, with a small hollow rattan ball and a net, similar to a tennis net. The aim is to get the ball over the net so that it touches down on the opposing team's side, within the court's boundaries. Sounds simple enough, but in takraw any part of the body can be used to keep the ball in the air and send it over the net *except* the hands and forearms. Feet, shins and ankles are most commonly used and many players compete bare-footed. Even village youngsters are sometimes extraordinarily skilled at the game, performing amazing athletic feats, almost similar to break-dancing, to keep the ball off the ground and return it over the net. Although there are rules and a scoring system they are often ignored in amateur matches, when performance, agility, style and spectator enjoyment all count for more. Another popular form of the sport is circle takraw, where a ring of players attempts to put the ball through a hoop suspended high above the centre of the circle, without letting the ball ever touch the ground.

Note 15, page 176: Strange goings-on

Although Songkran and some of Thailand's other national festivals are well known, there are other local celebrations and events which are hardly known at all, even to many Thais. Few visitors, and even the many long-term expat residents in the country, ever get to see them. Sometimes these local festivals are *so* local that they may take place only in one particular province, or even in just a few villages in the province. The celebrations are often fascinating, though their origins are sometimes obscure. Many have their roots in Brahmanism, Buddhism or animism but sometimes have elements of all three. Although often quite strange, they are always fun, always sanuk; an essential part of any Thai celebration.

Ghosts with human eyes: Considering how scared most Thai people are of ghosts, it's strange that there's a festival dedicated to them. But the *Phi Ta Khon Festival* has nothing to do with the specific and generally nasty ghosts I mentioned earlier. Instead, it's a fun and typically Thai mix of popular Buddhism and local animist traditions. Its Buddhist root is taken from one of the stories of the previous lives of the Buddha-to-be (the Chadok Tales) and the other is related to agrarian fertility and rain-making rites. The whole event is known locally as *Bun Luang*.

In Buddhist folklore, in a previous life the Buddha-to-be was born as Prince Vessandorn, a generous man who gave freely to others. One day he gave away a royal white elephant, which is revered as a symbol of rain. The local people were angry at the loss of the rare elephant from the city, thinking it would lead to drought and famine. They banished the prince into exile and he lived for many years as a hermit in the forest. Later, the king and the people forgave Vessandorn and invited him to return. He was welcomed back with a celebration so loud that even the dead woke up and joined in.

Bun Luang lasts three days and is held in June or July in the usually quiet little town of Dansai in Loei Province, about 450 kilometres north of Bangkok. The exact date for the festival is divined in advance by a local medium. Although celebrations include Buddhist religious and merit-making ceremonies, it's the processions, folk music, rockets and ghost masks that make it such an unusual and fun event.

Before dawn on the first day of the festival, the town medium and leaders perform a ceremony at the Mun River to invoke the spirit of the river, a legendary monk known as Phra Upakud. He's spent an eternity meditating beneath the water and has the form of a white marble sphere. His supernatural power and goodwill is needed to ensure that real ghosts don't take over the Phi Ta Khon Festival or linger on in the town afterwards.

After the invocation, breakfast is offered to monks at the local monastery but the festival really gets under way later in the day when thousands of people—mostly young men—dress in ghost costumes made from white shrouds or multi-coloured raggedy clothes. But it's the spectacular homemade masks that draw the crowds. The huge and elabourate masks are carved from the bases of coconut trees, then decorated with rice husks and coconut leaves before being hand-painted in brilliant colours and designs. Each mask has an elabourate wooden nose and may also have horns, buffalo bells or even a penis added to it, depending on the maker's imagination. The mask is always completed with a hat adapted from a bamboo basket of the kind usually used for cooking sticky rice. Some of the masks are so spectacular that folk museums around the world exhibit them and some have become collector's items.

The ghosts are joined by fearsome-looking 'mud-men'; near-naked youths covered from head to foot in thick, brown, dried mud. The ghost masks and costumes are beautiful but the mud-men—unadorned and without bright colour—are really quite scary-looking. Together, ghosts and mud-men parade and dance through the streets accompanied by loud music and large quantities of alcohol, while teasing the girls in the crowd with realistic phallic symbols, sometimes not very subtly disguised as swords, clubs and other weapons.

On the second day of the festival, the ghosts accompany a revered Buddha image through the town, while monks chant the story of Prince Vessandorn. At the end of the parade, huge homemade bamboo rockets are fired off to encourage the deities to send rain for a good harvest. Dance contests and sports events are held and there are prizes for the best ghost masks and costumes. Later, in a more subdued and sober mood, people gather at the local monastery to listen to Buddhist sermons, recited by the monks.

Traditionally, on the final day of the festival the ghost masks should be thrown into the river to send the demons back to the underworld, but in modern times entrepreneurial ghosts offer their masks for sale to visitors.

(Although the English translation of 'Phi Ta Khon' is now usually written as 'ghosts with human eyes', that may not be correct. The word '*phi*' means 'ghost' and the word '*ta*' means 'eye', but '*ta khon*' is 'eyelash'. The word '*khon*' on its own can mean 'person' or 'people', depending on the context, but if spoken in a different tone can mean 'mask' or 'body hair', but not head hair. Take your choice!)

The mysterious Nak fireballs: The strange annual *Nak* fireball show in Nong Khai, in Thailand's northeast, is an event which has started to attract international interest. Known locally as *Bangfai Phaya Nak*, the fireball show is a natural—or supernatural— phenomenon which has been occurring for hundreds and possibly thousands of years. On the full moon night of October, coinciding with the end of the three-month-long Buddhist Rains Retreat, dozens, hundreds and sometimes *thousands* of egg-size, ruby-coloured glowing balls rise from the surface of the murky Mekong River, float slowly to a height of up to one hundred metres and then disappear: no sound, no smell, no smoke. One year, more than 3,000 fireballs were seen. What are they?

Locals are adamant that the fireballs are shot or spit into the air by legendary Nak; huge serpent-like creatures that are the guardians of the river. In popular Buddhist mythology, during his final incarnation the Buddha visited his mother in one of the heavenly realms to preach to her. When he returned to Earth, he was welcomed back by the Nak, who blew fireballs into the sky.

There are many kinds of Nak in Buddhist and Hindu mythology and they usually have the form of a hooded snake, like a cobra, but are very much larger. They have magical powers and live under water or in deep caves in the earth, or even inside termite mounds. Representations of Nak can be seen in every monastery in Thailand, decorating the stairs leading up to the main temple doors.

Scientists don't like the locals' colourful explanation very much and have boringly suggested instead that the fireballs are caused by fermentation of organic sediment on the river bed, much like swamp gas. They claim that globules of methane and nitrogen rise to the surface of the water, combust spontaneously and float into the air, and it's just coincidence that it usually happens on the last night of the Rains Retreat. Other scientists disagree, saying that it's impossible for bubbles of gas to survive in the river's strong current. They usually agree, though, that the phenomenon is not a man-made hoax.

Whatever scientific explanations are put forward, locals remain firmly convinced that Nak exist in the river. Many people claim to have seen them swimming briefly on the surface or they have seen long trails left in the muddy river banks where a Nak has come ashore.

It is possible that very large serpent-like creatures do live in the depths of the Mekong, especially on the Laos side of the river, where the water is deeper. One may have been photographed. The famous but controversial photograph is of a group of US servicemen who were apparently stationed at a secret base in Laos in 1973. In the photograph about twenty men are holding a silvery eel-like fish, about eight metres long. Locals swear the photograph was taken in the Mekong region and that the fish is a Nak. Some scientists have said the strange fish could be an unknown species of eel, or even a gigantic snake called a Matsoid, thought to be extinct. Matsoids grew up to eighteen metres long and had crested heads—exactly what has been described by locals who claim to have seen a Nak.

According to the locals' story, the creature in the photograph was sent back to the US for scientific study but disappeared before it got there. They claim that all the servicemen in the photograph met with unfortunate deaths, as a result of taking the Nak from the river. The US Navy says that the photograph is genuine but was taken in 1996 on a Californian beach and shows a rarely seen, deep water creature called an Oarfish. That's a military cover-up, respond Nong Khai locals, since the photograph has been around a lot longer than that.

Regardless of the authenticity of the photograph or the various explanations for the fireball phenomenon, it's still one of the strangest sights to be seen in Thailand. I'm sure Granny had never heard of the event, but I'm also sure which explanation she would have preferred!

The Rocket Festival: Every mid-May, the skies above Yasothon Province in the northeast are filled with the noisy *whoosh* and *bang* of hundreds of homemade bamboo rockets, some of them enormous and climbing to heights of more than one kilometre. It's the time of the annual *Bun Bangfai* Rocket Festival; a colourful, exciting, bawdy and fun-filled two days for farmers hoping for a good rainy season and an abundant rice harvest— and doing anything they can to make that happen. May marks the end of the long, dry and very hot season when there may have been little or no rain for months, and precedes wetter weather and the beginning of the planting season. If the rains don't come exactly when they should, the rice and other crops may fail.

Near the end of the dry season, groups of villagers all over the province make their beautiful and elabourately decorated rockets, as much as nine metres long and filled with explosive black powder. The bigger the rocket, the higher it will go and the more pleased the sky gods will be. The rockets are transported from the villages to the city mounted on decorated buffalo carts or flat-bed trucks, which are also sometimes the rocket launch pads.

The festival is basically a fertility rite; a way of encouraging the male sky god to fertilise the female god of the earth with his rain and being prompted to do so by phallic rockets shot into his realm. The whole festival follows this bawdy theme. On the first day, the rockets are paraded through the city escorted by colourful dance troupes, musicians and floats. The procession makes its way to the City Pillar where the rocket makers pay homage to *Chao Pu,* the guardian spirit of the city. In the evening the streets are alive and noisy with a fair, parties, folk music and, oddly, drunken men staggering around dressed in women's clothes. On the second day, the rockets are again paraded before making their way to the launch area in a park on the edge of the city. Many young men and boys from farming families ordain temporarily as novice monks on the second day, hoping to make merit for their families, which will also help ensure a good harvest.

The rockets are finally launched, but interested by-standers shouldn't get too close because not all the rockets make a successful take off. Many simply fizzle out harmlessly but in 1999 a large one exploded a few seconds after it was launched, killing five people. If a rocket fails to launch or ignite at all, the maker is thrown into a mud pool. By examining the trajectories of the rockets and the cloud formations they pass through, local seers can predict whether the coming growing season will be bountiful or not.

The festival has been held for hundreds of years but in recent times has been brought up to date with the addition of a Miss Bun

Bangfai beauty contest, traditional dance shows, open air theatre and live folk music. Considerable amounts of rice whisky are also consumed.

A grisly food fest: A vegetarian food festival doesn't sound particularly interesting—unless you're a vegetarian—but the annual *Ngan Kin Che* festival held in late September or early October in Phuket is not only interesting, it's positively bizarre. It's also a bit gruesome and definitely not for the faint-hearted.

Since the early ninteenth century, many Chinese and Thai-Chinese people on the Southern island of Phuket have become very strict vegetarians for ten days during the ninth lunar month of the Chinese calendar. But they don't only stop eating meat; they also give up sex, alcohol, smoking, swearing, killing animals and even wearing jewellery. As if that's not enough of a penance many devotees, in self-induced religious trances, stick swords, knives, skewers, *fish*—just about anything—through their cheeks and tongues and then walk on burning coals, all without apparent pain, injury or even significant loss of blood. The rituals and extreme self-mutilation are believed to cleanse the body and mind while also showing the power of the devotees' religious faith. These devotees, or mediums, are known as *Ma Song* (Entranced Horses) and they allow themselves to be possessed by the gods, who protect them from harm while they perform their acts of horrific self-mutilation.

The devotees, with their astonishing and spectacular array of sharp instruments through cheeks and tongues, parade through the town, where householders and traders set up tables of offerings, including tiny cups of tea and other gifts for the gods in the persona of the pierced Ma Song. The Ma Song give blessings for good luck and prosperity in return. They may hang some of the gifts from the various implements piercing their faces before continuing their progress through the town.

Although the festival is known mainly as a vegetarian food festival (and the streets are full of stalls selling only vegetarian food) it's primarily a religious celebration. It's the Festival of the Nine Emperor Gods, which celebrates the return to earth of the spirits of nine Emperors, representing health, wealth and prosperity. The gods are summoned back to earth each year to witness the incredible display of faith by their followers. The gods are invoked in a religious ceremony at the start of the festival and return to earth by way of tall poles hung with lanterns, erected at the town's most important Chinese temples. Religious ceremonies are held at temples and shrines throughout the festival by white-clad devotees who offer gifts of incense, candles and food, and seek blessings from the gods in return. At the end of the festival, the gods are sent back to their heavenly realm with religious ceremonies, colourful and noisy parades, cultural performances and fabulous rocket displays.

The festival originated in 1825 when an opera troupe from China visited the island to entertain the many Chinese people working in local tin mines. All the members of the troupe fell mysteriously ill—possibly from malaria—which they believed was caused by their failure to pay enough respect to the gods. They recovered from their illness after adopting a strict vegetarian diet and holding ceremonies to appease their deities. Local people, impressed by the troupes' recovery, embraced the cult (known locally as *Kao Wang Che*) from which the present festival has developed.

Burning Boats: On the full moon night of October, on the last day of the Buddhist Rains Retreat, the Mekong River at Nakhon

Phanom in the northeast is lit up by spectacular hand-crafted boats, brightly burning as they float majestically on the dark water. These aren't crude model boats; some are ten metres long and are of fantastic and elabourate designs, depicting creatures and events from Buddhist and Hindu mythology, as well as animist folklore themes. The burning boats carry offerings of sticky rice, sweets and other food and are adorned with flowers, incense and candles, as well as spectacular fireworks and pyrotechnics.

Many Thai festivals are concerned with rain-making, but the Boats of Fire Festival—*Lai Ruea Fai*—is held to give thanks to several deities for the water received during the rainy season, or for water taken and used from the river during the year. Local tradition has it that the festival commemorates the same event in Buddhist mythology that the Nak fireballs celebrate; the return to Earth of the Buddha after spending three months in a heavenly realm preaching to his mother. The festivals' pre-Buddhist Hindu roots can be found in veneration of the Nak, the guardian serpent who rules over rivers. Its animist elements are in the worship of various deities associated with water and fertility: *Mae* (the Life Mother), *Mae Phra Thorani* (the Earth Mother,) *Mae Phosop* (the Rice Mother) and *Mae Khong Kha* (the Mother of the Waters) who lives in and protects rivers.

The festival has been held for many generations but originally in a much simpler form, with boats made from the trunks of banana trees or bamboo, and without modern pyrotechnics. It's only in recent years that it has become so spectacular and has grown to include street parades and other celebrations.

Monkey business: According to an ancient Indian legend, the Ramayana, the Hindu deity Rama sought the help of the monkey king, Hanuman, to rescue Rama's wife, who had been kidnapped

233

by the demon-king Ravana. Hanuman led his army of monkeys in a great victory over the demon-king. As a reward, Rama decided to create a new city to be ruled by the monkey king. To choose the location, he fired a magic arrow into the air and built the city where the arrow landed.

In Thailand's own version of the story, the Ramakien, that city is Lopburi, in the central region. Originally called Lawo, the city is more than 1,000 years old, though there were Bronze Age settlements in the area more than 3,500 years ago. Today, many Lopburi locals believe that the huge Macaque monkey population living happily amongst them in the ruins of a Khmer temple in the city centre are the descendants of Hanuman. Estimates of the monkey population range from 600 to more than 1,000. Once a year, on the last weekend in November, they are treated like kings, with a huge feast.

Although the monkeys have lived in the city for hundreds of years, the monkey feast itself originated only in the late 1980s when (the story goes) a local hotel owner, wanting to improve his business, implored Hanuman for help. His business subsequently improved and he repaid his debt by offering the first feast to the monkey king's descendants. And what a feast! Nowadays, several thousand kilos of food are laid out in the Khmer ruins in spectacular and colourful displays on huge tables. On the menu are fresh fruit, vegetables, boiled eggs, sticky rice, cookies, ice cream and jelly, as well as cans of fruit juice and fizzy drinks. When the feast starts, it's an eating frenzy; these monkeys have very poor table manners.

The Lopburi monkeys have totally adapted to urban living. They stroll casually and without fear along the busy streets, sit around on the pavements or on parked cars and motorcycles, and pop into local shops, stealing anything that isn't nailed down. They even look carefully before crossing the roads, though locals drive very slowly through the centre of town because to injure a monkey would be considered very unlucky. If a monkey is injured for any reason, the town has its own little monkey hospital. Locals claim the monkeys even go on day trips, sitting on the roof of trains leaving from Lopburi railway station in the morning and returning in the evening. Some say the monkeys make these excursions to fight rival gangs of monkeys in other towns.

Local people are generally very tolerant of the monkeys. Although they are mischievous and cause some damage, the monkeys attract many thousands of visitors each year to what is an otherwise fairly ordinary provincial city. But visitors should be careful. The young monkeys are especially cute and enjoy climbing onto visitors' shoulders, but these are street-wise kids and will steal anything they can get their little hands on, scampering off with glasses, handbags, cameras and jewellery.

Note 16, page 179: *The Rains Retreat*

Thousands of young Thai men become monks for the duration of the three-month-long rainy season. Ordaining for even such a short time gives them the opportunity to learn the basics of the Buddha's teaching and they can also pass on the merit earned from ordaining to their parents, as a way of thanking them for their love and care.

Khao Phansa or *Vassa*, the rainy season retreat, was an established practice in India long before the time of the Buddha. At the start of the rainy season, monks and ascetics of many religious philosophies took up residence in a particular place and stayed there until the monsoon season had passed. There were practical reasons for doing so. Much of the low-lying land was flooded and what tracks or roads existed were frequently washed away, making the monks' traditional wandering life impossible.

When the Buddha established his order of monks he made no rule against them continuing their wanderings during the monsoon period. Some of his disciples asked the Buddha if it was right that ascetics of other religions stopped travelling during the wet season while Buddhist monks continued their travels 'crushing green herbs, hurting vegetable life and destroying the life of many small things'. The Buddha agreed that it wasn't right and told the monks that they should cease their wanderings during that period.

The purpose of the Buddha's decree was not just so that his monks would cease damaging crops but also to give them a fixed period for study, meditation and to teach newer monks. Although in modern times monks could travel regardless of the weather and without damaging crops, the tradition of the Phansa as a period of study and intensified practice remains.

An appeal on behalf
of needy Thai youngsters

In 1994, when he was the monk Phra Peter Pannapadipo, co-author Peter Robinson established a fund to help one particularly impoverished Thai youngster who had gained a university place but couldn't afford the fees. Peter's friends in the UK donated money to help but gave more than enough, so the balance became the foundation of a trust fund (then the Students' Education Trust), dedicated to helping other disadvantaged students in similar difficulties. The original student is now a Doctor of Nuclear Physics.

By the end of 2009, the charity—by then The SET Foundation—was supporting 1,200 students at high school, college and university and had awarded in total more than 3,500 scholarships.

Most SET-supported students are from very poor rice-farming families. Without SET's help, most of the older students would have been unable to take up their deserved college or university places. Some of those already in vocational or tertiary education—or even at high school—would have been forced to drop out and return to work in the family rice paddies or seek some other mundane, dead-end job. With SET's support, the students are *achieving;* achieving something for themselves, for their families and for the future of their country.

SET helps students in different ways, depending on individual need. For example:

- New students who have passed entrance examinations for college or university but who cannot take up their places because of proven family poverty.
- Students already in higher education who may be forced to drop out, unable to afford further fees or expenses.
- Students who need financial help of some other kind— for books, uniform, tools, spectacles, canteen lunch, bus fares or dormitory accommodation. Some particularly impoverished students may need total support.

Whatever genuine help the student needs, SET tries to provide it

SET students at university currently receive annual scholarships of 20,000 baht, while those at vocational colleges receive 12,000 baht. High school students receive 6,000 baht per year. Additional welfare grants can be made depending on individual proven need and after approval by the university, college or school welfare department. SET works closely with welfare officers and teachers to ensure that all students who are supported meet SET's dual criteria of *proven need plus proven diligence*.

Tertiary and higher vocational training in Thailand is relatively inexpensive but there are thousands of bright, diligent and deserving youngsters who cannot afford even the modest fees and expenses. A small donation goes a long way in education in Thailand and can make a genuine and *immediate* difference to the future of a bright boy or girl.

For more information about SET's work, please visit the website: *www.thaistudentcharity.org*.